THE DALAI LAMA

Burma's internal conflict in the past several decades has had a drastic impact on the lives of its people. "Children of the Revolution" is an encouraging account of a Burmese monk's effort to alleviate their plight, especially that of the children.

The author, Feroze Dada, gives a moving account of the monk's work and talks about his own efforts to support a school and a care centre for destitute Burmese children started by the monk in his monastery. I offer my prayers for their success.

September 18, 2014

The story of the Children of the Revolution concludes in part three of the book which can be downloaded free of charge from www.inletrust.org.uk

We were travelling in a small
boat on Inle Lake in Burma
when a freak storm hit the lake.
We put ashore in the village of Phaya Taung
and were given shelter by the monks.
What happened next changed our lives.
It could change yours...

Every morning we are born again.
What we do today is what matters most.

Buddha

THis is a True Story

...about a Burmese freedom fighter, a monk and 600 abandoned children.

It's about our journey together against the backdrop of a beautiful and remote lake community in what has been one of the most turbulent and dangerous regions of the country now called Myanmar.

It begins with my own journey of discovery. I first went to Myanmar in 2009 twenty years after the military rulers decided to change the name from Burma to rid the country of what they saw as the last vestiges of its colonial past.

Like most journeys, I found myself setting off for one destination only to arrive at another. I thought I was writing one story only to discover that there were deeper layers that I hadn't uncovered yet. I thought I was writing about one man, only to meet another.

Each encounter brought me closer to discovering something new about myself. I was beginning to turn the pages on a new and exciting chapter in my own life.

Feroze

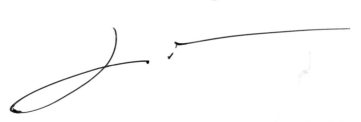

MAP OF INLE, SAMKAR & KAKKU REGION

N
W — GIC — E
S

Kalaw · Aung Ban · Heho · Shwe Nyaung · Taung Gyi
Ta Nang Ray
Panta Kwar
Dat Daw · Nyaung Shwe · Lwe Kaung
Hopone
Yea Cho
Kone Ni · Nar Baung
Mya Thein Tan · Loi Khaw · Hti Ham Swe
Inle Spa · Maing Thauk · Naung Kar
Myin Ma Ti · Kaung Daing · Rest House · Pon Tae · Ta Khaw Mu · Nam Kook
Pin Mi · Lin Kin · Loi Lam · Yan Aung
Kye Sar Gone · Naung Lay · Inn Ne Mt · Hti Phaung
Hti-Tain · Namrop · Kon Shen · Tha Pyay Gone · Won Ya
Pae Tu Pauk · Hti Ling · Thale-U · Hmwe Taw · Hti wa mu
Nang Thein · Ye Kaung To · Nga Phe Chaung · Dat Daw Ya Do · Hti Not · Ham See
Ywa Mah · Phaung Daw Oo · Kae Taung · Thu Tan
Mine Lone · TaungKa Mauk · Pagoda · Ma Gyi Pin · Hti Rea · Kyaung Hti
In Dein · Nampan · Moe Kaung · Mai Law · Loi leik · Naung Mon
Ti Kyit · Se Kaung · Chaung Par · Kae Lu · Hti tat · Kakku
In Paw Khon · Dong ta khawh · Hlaing Konn Restaurant
Kwe Thaung · U Daung Taung · Kye Paw Khon · Loi Khaw · Dat Gyi · Hti Ne · Ta Nang Htaw
Tha Pyay · Mine Pyo · Phayani · Ye Cho · Naung Kei · Ban Yin
In Kyin Gone · Hae Lone · Ka Naing Gyi · Nam Hu
Se Sone · Tat Lot · Lone Gone · Naung Ya Sai
Ti Pong · Ma Gyi Seik · Loi Maw · Hti Ta Maung · Saung Phoe · Loi Saung · Nam Hu
Taung Toe · Hti Plun
Myay Phyu · Kyaine Kam · Loi Kam
Pain Nae Gone · Kyauk Daing · Taung Che · Lwe Sam Sip
Myay Cha · Pan Kan
Water Fall · Kyauk Ta Lone
Ponmu · Kon Sin · Kon Maw · Ti Pone
Naung Tayar · Hti Ree · Baung · Bun Pyin · Kyauk Ta Lone Nge · Phlit Pon · Naung Hein Pay
Mawbe Market · Hti Kham · Mae Ton · Naung Hein Gyi · Seik Khao
Mawbe Bridge · Ham Nyar · Pin Tonn
Thapyay Gone
Naung Pi · Nam Hu · Kaung Nain Mt
Li Me · Ti Kaung · Hti Kwa · Hti ta Maung
Pyet Hee
Nar Mon · Loi Kawe · Pone Faim
Naung Bo · Nam Tek
Lwe Mon · Carya
Tar Kaung · Sae Khaung · Pain Pone · Ta Vee Pion · War Cra
Pin Long · Thaya gona · Samkar · Loi lon
Ti ta kawh
Kone Tha · Se Seing
Te wa mu
Lont Kant · Phaya Taung
Hsi Pin Kauk
Maine U.
Nam Tote Market
Saung Plaung
Lwe Pen Boh · Lwe Paw

(Legend)
- Trekking Road
- Permanent Road
- River / Creek / Lake
- Pass
- Railway Line
- Airport

About the Author

Feroze Dada was born in Karachi. He has lived and worked for most of his life in London.

He is a qualified chartered accountant and chartered tax advisor. He was the senior partner of his private client tax practice for 30 years and is currently chairman of Crowe Clarke Whitehill office in Mayfair. He is also a non-executive director of several private companies. Outside his professional life, Feroze is passionate about cricket and music. He currently performs in his own band, the Tax Pistols. This is his first book but hopefully not his last.

MuMu (Farida) Dada - Photographer, interpreter and guide.

MuMu was born in Taunggyi, Burma and then lived in Karachi. She currently runs the family's property business in London.

MuMu and Feroze met in London and were married in Pakistan. They have two grown up children, Sumaya and Nadir, and divide their time between their homes in London and Italy.

What people are saying about the book

"This deeply moving book comprises many tales which all help to tell the wider story of a troubled country. These stories, along with vivid descriptions of the land and its peoples, form the backdrop to one of the most inspiring narratives I have read in a long time: the author's quest to help a monastery school become self-sufficient. His determination and compassion shine from the pages.

With so much going on this could be a confusing read, but Feroze has structured the story well and his excellent photos help to set the scene more fully. It's a good read and a wonderful story; I hope it will succeed in its fundraising aims."

Jane Mallin - Reviewer

"It is a true story that combines politics, religion, travel, adventure and self-discovery. One of the most unexpected things about it is that the author is a chartered accountant living in London! This is his first book and it turns out that he is a natural writer. It is beautifully written in a prose that is simple, direct and elegant.

The story draws the reader in from the first page and is full of surprises -- as well as unforgettable characters (such as Major and the Monk). Furthermore, the entire manuscript is illustrated with gorgeous photography."

Dr. Brian Klug. Senior Research Fellow in Philosophy.
Oxford University

"Set against Burma's long and violent struggle for freedom, the author has captured a powerful and compelling story of heroism and hope. At its heart is a personal and often moving journey which will inspire all who read it."

Andrew Thorman Radio & Television Journalist

"Viewed through the eyes of a freedom fighter struggling against feudalism and a Buddhist monk determined to build a future for children orphaned through war and disease, Dada sensitively builds a many-layered picture of a country struggling to come to terms with democracy while at the same time losing its innocence in the face of a surge of capitalism.

But this is not simply a book about Myanmar's journey towards a new freedom, with all of the complexity that freedom brings. It is also a story of the author's own journeys: as a Muslim absorbing Buddhist philosophy and as a London tax accountant who finds new meanings in his life by launching a charity that will bring education and hope to thousands of Burmese children.

It is a journey that every reader will urge him to complete."

Nigel Carrington
Vice-Chancellor of University of the Arts

This is a current day story interposed with the history of Burma and how little it has been allowed to progress since independence. The author seems to personify the generosity of spirit which somehow has managed to survive in Burma. The book resonates with humanity but also urgent achievement when opportunities brought by outsiders are patiently developed.

This book is a triumph of character defined by action. The personalities at the heart of this book have stories to tell that are worthy of world-wide celebration."

Professor Alan Richardson
Ri Chair of Science in Enterprise

"Words do not express thoughts
very well; every thing immediately
becomes a little different,
a little distorted,
a little foolish.
And yet it also pleases me and seems
right that what is of value and wisdom
of one man seems
non sense to another."

Buddha

Acknowledgements

My sincere thanks to Andrew Thorman, Chris Day, and Jane Mallin for having the wisdom to make sense of my writing and to my wife MuMu Farida for painting my thoughts so beautifully with her photographs.

To my parents Ahmad & Halima Dada and my brother Captain Siraj Dada for their spiritual guidance and prayers.

My thanks to so many who already have and those in the future who continue to help The Inle Trust to fulfil its charitable objectives.

But above all my admiration for the children at Phaya Taung monastery who through their dignity and humility have been the true inspiration for this book.

"We are what we think.
All that we are
arises with
our thoughts.
With our thoughts,
we make
the world."

Buddha

Children
of the
Revolution

Feroze Dada

Published by
Filament Publishing Ltd
16, Croydon Road, Waddon, Croydon,
Surrey, CR0 4PA, United Kingdom
Telephone +44 (0)20 8688 2598
Fax +44 (0)20 7183 7186
info@filamentpublishing.com
www.filamentpublishing.com

ISBN - 978-1-910125-14-4

Printed by Berforts Information Press

Editors: Andrew Thorman Jane Mallin
Layout and Design: Chris Day

All the profits from this book belong to The Inle Trust
Charity Registered in England Number 1154767
www.inletrust.org.uk

Contents

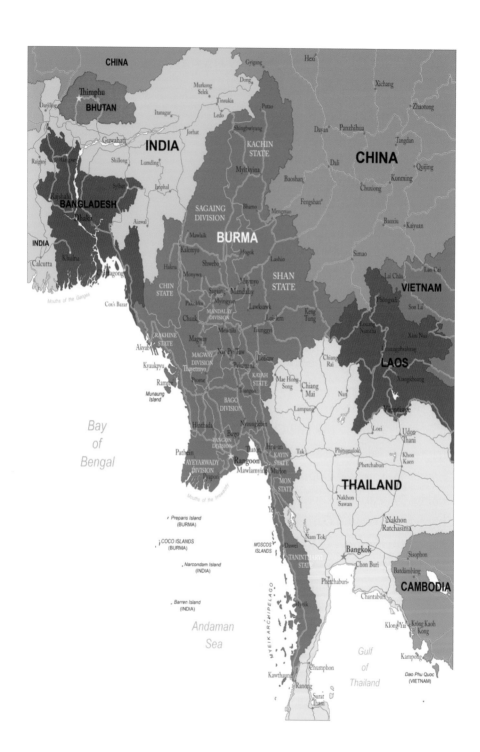

The Story Begins

My story begins with my own journey of discovery. I first went to Myanmar in 2009 – twenty years after the military rulers decided to change the name from Burma to rid the country of what they saw as the last vestiges of its colonial past.

I went there to meet my wife's family and in the course of exploring the country we chanced upon what was then a remote and beautiful lake. It was here I encountered Major, one of the most remarkable people I have ever met. And I promised to write his story.

In the following years I made several return visits to record his story, often secretly, and in the course of our growing friendship I discovered a new trust and belief, which has also changed my life.

Like most journeys, I found myself setting off for one destination only to arrive at another. I thought I was writing one story only to discover that there were deeper layers that I hadn't uncovered yet. I thought I was writing about one man, only to meet another. Each encounter brought me closer to discovering something new about myself. I was beginning to turn the pages on a new and exciting chapter in my own life.

Myanmar: troubled past, uncertain future

It's thought there are at least one and half million orphans in Myanmar – formerly Burma. A country whose inner beauty has been scarred by the ravages of conflict throughout its troubled history.

Myanmar is struggling to come to terms with the democratic process. Though free elections took place in 2010, after fifty years of military rule deep cultural and religious divisions remain. The new President Thein Sein promised greater freedom for his people. He won international acclaim by freeing Aung San Suu Kyi – known as 'the Lady' – after years of house arrest and he opened up the country to the outside world again. The international community responded in kind. The US and European Union dropped all non-military sanctions and promised development aid. President Obama visited and invited Thein Sein to the White House. Despite this, Burma remains a fragile and volatile country with more than 135 ethnic tribes.

The Burman people, who make up around 68% of the 48 million population, dominate these groups. Others include the Karen, Shan and Rakhine. Military offensives to quell years of separatist rebellions officially ended with ceasefires in 2011 and 2012.

But beneath its placid waters lurks a dangerous current of resentment, suspicion and feudal rivalry. A deep simmering mistrust between Buddhists and Muslims sparked renewed violence. Now the world watches and holds its breath.

This extraordinary country of contrasts, this beautiful lush landscape of mountains, jungle and rivers is at a crossroads. Rich in natural resources including timber, oil, gas and rice as well as a source of many precious stones such as rubies and sapphires, the economy is one of the least developed in the world. Corruption is rife as is large scale trafficking in heroin.

There are many reasons why Myanmar has so many abandoned children. Conflict yes, but also poverty, disease – particularly malaria and TB – and natural disasters such as the devastating cyclone that struck the country in 2008 claiming at least 140,000 lives.

This story is about just some of them and some of the remarkable people who have devoted their lives to helping them.

All the profits from this book will be donated to the monastery school and orphanage at Inle, Phaya Taung.
www.inletrust.org.uk

Lake Inle

"You have a fascinating story to tell.

Will you let me write it?" I asked.

Major thought for a moment

then looked at me with a slight smile.

"I am afraid that the government

will not like that at all..."

Part One

Chapter 1: Rebel with a Cause

There was something about him that stood out. He had a distinctive, almost superior look. Bold and confident. He commanded attention. He had, I would definitely say, an air of authority.

He was probably in his mid-fifties, of average Burmese build, short and lean by European standards, but he exuded great presence.

I began talking to him. It turned out that he knew this place – in fact he knew everyone. He was warm and friendly as he smiled and greeted us; there was a slight air of diffidence, almost as though he felt humbled in our presence. At the same time I knew that the smiling man in front of me had led a very different past.

He sat talking with my wife MuMu and our children, Sumaya and Nadir. He'd previously met MuMu on an earlier visit. But this was the first time I'd met him.

His name was Major and he was a rebel. As I got to know him I learned that he'd spent years fighting the military government. He'd been shot. He'd seen terrible things.

He'd now chosen to take a different path.

We chatted for a while before I decided to take a risk and cut to the chase. I wanted to know about his days as a guerrilla fighting the Burmese establishment. I waited for him to change the subject but, far from being coy, he was eager to share his story. It was, it seemed, a kind of catharsis for him.

So Major began to tell the story of his life. There were none of those hesitations and corrections that most of us make when we speak about complex or painful experiences: it was almost as though he was reading from a book or a script or as though he had fallen into a trance. He held my attention completely.

His father, a rebel just as his son would one day become, was killed by the establishment he had fought against so ardently when Major was six years old. Major went on to join the Pa'O movement at the age of 21; the earliest age that he would be allowed to fight.

Suddenly he stopped talking. After a pause, he lowered his voice and said, "I am sorry. They do not like me talking so frankly about my past." Looking up, I saw a waiter nudging ever closer to our table and listening to every word Major said.

There are government observers everywhere in Myanmar; in hotels, restaurants – especially the ones that foreigners frequent. They keep their eyes and ears open and report anything deemed unusual. After a while it's easy to spot these 'spies' because they make no attempt at subtlety.
All the locals know who they are because they tend to stand around pretending to be busy while not actually doing anything; other than eavesdropping that is.

"You have a fascinating story to tell. Will you let me write it?" I asked.

Major thought for a moment then looked at me with a slight smile. "I am afraid that the government will not like that at all…"

"Three things cannot
be long hidden:
the sun, the moon,
and the truth."

Buddha

He turned towards me
and gently squeezing
my hand, he said:
"I just wanted to tell you that
if you go to the lake
it will change your
life completely."

Chapter 2: The Arrival

"When I met my wife MuMu Maung she was like a beautiful Burmese flower – I wondered where she came from and after meeting her parents I realised that it was from a strong and loving family tree. I have now had the pleasure of meeting the rest of her family here in Taunggyi and I realise their roots are deep, honest and faithful... Thank you all so much for making us so welcome."

I was making a speech to MuMu's family at a party they'd arranged for us – MuMu, Sumaya, Nadir and myself – in honour of our first visit to Myanmar. It was 2009.

The entire Maung clan – all 54 first cousins, most of whom still live in Taunggyi – turned up for the barbecue. They brought mountains of delicious food and drink, including a lethal homemade rice-based wine as well as some very pleasant chardonnay from a local vineyard. The younger boys had brought guitars, drums and an accordion. It was a moonlit winter's evening and as the sun began to set it became quite cold.

The wine flowed as the band played a selection of popular English songs from the Fifties and Sixties. Everyone joined in the sing-song and we all held hands and danced around the roaring fire. It was a truly emotional and touching reunion.

Ahwin Kaw Kaw, the eldest member of the Maung clan, was nominated to say a few words in reply to my thank you speech.

I had spent much of my time that evening talking to him. About 80, he was a short man with a heavily lined face. He stood absolutely upright and appeared healthy and strong. He exuded a magnetic serenity. I asked him what the secret of his contentment was.

"I have very little but I need even less."

"But Ahwin," I said. "I meant the spiritual context."

He gave me a wry smile. "I do mean spiritually. I am content just to be alive and I thank God for every day that he gives me."

Although hugely respected by the family Ahwin had caused something of an upset by marrying a Christian after the death of his first wife. The older Maung clan were all devout Muslims. But his patience and kindness had eventually won them over.

He stood up to welcome us. "The tree can only be as strong as the love and nourishment it gets," he said. "MuMu, you have come here all the way from London and have brought your family with you; this is the food our family tree needs to become even stronger."

As the evening drew to an end Ahwin took me to one side. "It would be really nice if you could spend a few minutes with me tomorrow, I have a message for you."

I was up fairly early the next morning and decided to walk from the hotel to his house, which was only 10 minutes away.

Ahwin was sitting outside on the porch drinking tea. He got up and shook my hand and, gesturing for me to sit in the chair next to him, poured me a cup of strong milky sweet tea.

We chatted for a while and he told me how much he liked MuMu's parents and how close he was to her mother, MayMay. He was also very pleased that I had married MuMu, who was one of his favourite cousins. Then he turned towards me and gently squeezing my hand, he said:

"I just wanted to tell you that if you go to the lake it will change your life completely."

He didn't expand on his thoughts and reverted to small talk again. But I couldn't leave it there. What had he meant? His expression suggested he did not wish to say anything further, not then anyway, so I let it go.

That afternoon we were invited to cousin Ting's house for a private lunch. He lives in a very posh residential part of Taunggyi, his house perched on the hilltop overlooking, yet secluded from, the town centre. Cousin Ting is rather highbrow – a well-known local architect married to a Shan princess who also happens to be a GP and who thus ticks all the right boxes in qualifying as 'upper class' in local Shan society.

It was an impressive lunch too. There were at least twenty different dishes. As was customary, neither Ting nor his wife sat with us but stood around and served us (as did several domestic helpers) as we ate, replenishing our plates with virtually every mouthful consumed.

After lunch we discussed our tentative plans for the next few days but Ting abruptly announced that he had planned a surprise excursion. A trip to Inle Lake! I couldn't believe it coming so quickly after Ahwin's prediction.

So the next morning we set off for the three hour drive to the lake. Cousin Ting and his wife Sabai had arranged for us to stay with them as their guests at a hotel owned by Ting's client on a remote part of the lake. Some years ago, Ting had stepped in to complete the building after the previous architect had suddenly died.

In gratitude Ting always had a place to holiday whenever he wanted. He continued to visit and helped advise on the structural maintenance of the hotel while Sabai held free surgeries for the local families.

Sabai always looked rather sad. Ting explained how they had met at school. She'd had a very tragic upbringing. Her grandfather had been a raja within the Shan State and her father, a politician, had fought for a federal Shan state side by side with the famous PNO leader Bo Kyaw against the Ne Win military government. Sabai's brother had been killed in the fighting and both her parents were rumoured to have been murdered by the opposition regime. Sabai had cried endlessly in school. Ting vowed to marry her and promised that he would never make her cry. He kept both promises.

As there wasn't enough room in Ting's car for the four of us, Cousin Ngni Ngni insisted that he and cousin Stanley would drive us to the lake.

They had planned a picnic en route and to stop for a few beers at the hot springs on the way back after dropping us off. Ngni Ngni was instantly likeable, a friendly and happy man who was genuinely loved by everyone. Unusually for a Burmese, he was tall, well-built and apparently something of an accomplished sportsman having played basketball for his country! He now worked as a coach at the local golf and country club.

I asked him what he thought of Ahwin's comments about the lake changing my life. "Ahwin is truly a remarkable man," he said "a palmist and clairvoyant. But he stopped exercising his special gift because he believes foretelling the future (whether good or bad) interferes with the natural balance of life and therefore cannot be helpful. So what he said to you about going to the lake was very special."

Ting's car was something else, a white two-seater made from parts of a Ford and a Nissan. He called it his Aston Martin. Ngni Ngni turned up exactly on time in something altogether more familiar, a van owned by someone called Stanley. Stanley, we were later told, was in the bicycle spare parts business – I later gathered that this meant he smuggled parts across the border from China.

So off we set towards Lake Inle. MuMu insisted that the very least we could do was to pay for the cost of filling up the van with petrol. We sped through several villages and suddenly Stanley stopped the van and backed up under a tree where a few cars were parked near a large steel container drum. This was the petrol station – Myanmar style!

We drove for one hour or so; the landscape began to change, most of the sparsely scattered houses were on stilts and made of wood and woven bamboo.

We realised we were reaching the outskirts of the lake and that the houses here had to cater for living both on land and on water depending on the water level of the lake.

We were stopped unexpectedly by some soldiers standing by what looked like a checkpoint adjacent to a bunker. They were collecting entrance fees from tourists. Ngni Ngni refused to pay for MuMu on the grounds that that she was a local and in the end the soldiers gave way. This type of local collection was quite common, and I am sure it was a way for the soldiers to supplement their pay.

Arriving at the shore we then had to transfer to a boat for the journey to the hotel. When I say boat, I mean a canoe. Thankfully this one was fitted with an outboard. The six of us sat one behind the other along with two crew. It would take a further two hours to get to the hotel.

As we were about to set off, Ting handed us some bird feed and explained that we were about to witness one of nature's most remarkable shows.

This part of the lake was alive with activity, being the main mooring for both the tourist boats and also the main supply point for the various hotels and villages.

Local vendors were out in force selling everything from drinks and fruit to sun hats. But there was no shoving and pushing or hard sell as we're used to in many other countries. This was all very polite and calm – rather like, thank goodness, the water we were about to cross.

No sooner were we off than we were greeted by a flock of white birds. They swooped and dived over our heads and put on an amazing aerobatic display in the hope and expectation of a reward – hence the birdseed. It was a well-rehearsed performance, there was great skill in the way they cavorted and competed with each other to catch the feed and the birds were never threatening or demanding.

The spectacular aerial show lasted for at least fifteen minutes. Like a symphony, it reached its finale and the birds flew away together in the same way that they had arrived.

After two hours or so we approached a cluster of water cottages. As the boat reached the hotel reception area the hotel staff, all lined up in their immaculate uniforms, greeted us, smiling, ringing bells and banging gongs. We felt humbled and genuinely welcome.

After a cup of warm green tea we were whisked to our respective rooms. Our bungalow was sparsely furnished in natural wood, mainly bamboo with teak furniture.

There was a generous bathroom and veranda. It felt comfortable and was in total keeping with the lake surrounds. Ting had organised a special late lunch so we hurried back to reception where a table had been laid out. It was a very hot day and the cold beer added to the elation I already felt because of the beautiful surroundings.

Dusk was approaching and we went to our bungalows to change for the evening. The view from the veranda was captivating. The day was rapidly drawing to a close as was the activity on the lake. The sound of the water lapping the shore was now louder than the outboard engines of the fishing boats; clearly night was taking over from day.

The sunset over the lake took my breath away. I was reminded of a quote from Burmese Days by George Orwell: "Beauty is meaningless until it is shared." I agreed – but beauty like this could only be shared with its creator. We spent New Year's Eve together on the lake. The management and staff (and some guests) put on a dance and music show using a makeshift stage fitted to a barge that had been moored close by. The show culminated with fireworks at midnight.

We spent the evening with Major and his wife. The red wine we had picked up from the vineyard en route was a real treat but ran out very quickly so Ting and I resorted to the local rice wine, which kept us well oiled!

I was touched by how the locals had surrounded the hotel and the stage in their fishing boats. We invited them to join us because this was also their home and they made it work for us as we were now hopefully making it work for them.

Major disappeared the next day and so I didn't get the chance to pick up on where we'd left his story. I hadn't thought much about it at the time but we had been questioned in some detail by the authorities about our visit to Inle – far more so than about our proposed trip to the coast which was in a far more troublesome area. I wondered if it had something to do with Major.

Before we headed for the coast there was time to explore the area around Inle. Major had organized a boat trip to cover the local attractions and many traditional craft workshops. Although very touristy it provided a great introduction to the lake and its community and prepared us for the remote and awesome locations which await the more persistent and intrepid traveller.

There were all the usual shops selling clothing, silverware and jewellery, lacquer-ware and tobacco. The women were adept at making bamboo hats. Silk-weaving is another important industry, producing high-quality hand-woven and distinctive fabrics called 'longyis' – traditional sarongs.

The lotus plants that grow on the lake produce a unique fibre used to weave the special saffron robes worn by the monks. Needless to say, as commercial interests begin to exploit every possible opportunity, these are now sold to the public.

It takes one month and four thousand lotus stems to make just one scarf which then sells for around $300. That's a princely sum when the average annual income in Myanmar is less than $200.

The most famous image of the lake though is probably that of the leg-oarsmen who, with extraordinary dexterity, manage to glide their fishing boats across the water standing on one leg while using the other to propel their boat. The reason for this is actually quite simple – and typically practical. If they remain seated they can't see where they're going because of the vegetation that covers vast areas of the lake's surface!

Leg rowing oarsman on Lake Inle

Another abiding image associated with Burma is that of the Padaung women who elongate their necks by wearing a succession of gold or copper rings. The Padaung traditionally live along the Thai border. Sadly these beautifully adorned women are now more often employed as tourist attractions.

Legend has it that when the Padaung moved from China to settle in the jungle regions of North Eastern Burma there were many tigers and wild animals and in order to protect their women, the tribesmen wrapped them with golden helical rings.

These days gold has been replaced by brass and the rings restricted to their necks. They are seen as symbols of beauty. Usually the first rings are placed at the age of five and are consistently added to until they number sixteen by which time the neck has reached its maximum elongation of some twenty-five centimetres.

Also worth visiting is the Burmese cat sanctuary. Paradoxically, Burmese cats are virtually extinct in Myanmar.

This cat sanctuary has acquired the best possible pedigree stock from the UK and Australia as part of a breeding programme for the repopulation of these cats in different parts of Myanmar.

So, after our tourist diversion, it was off to Ngapali beach. The flight from He Ho to Thandwe airport in Rakhine State took about an hour. The beach is about four miles from the town of Thandwe (Sandoway). It is the most famous beach in Myanmar and a popular tourist destination.

It is also not far from an area where some of the most violent clashes between Muslims and Buddhists have taken place. Because of this Ngapali is not as well publicised as other beaches in South East Asia but, in my view, ranks among the very best and boasts some luxurious hotels.

Its beautiful sandy beach stretches for three kilometres along the Indian Ocean in the Bay of Bengal. Ngapali is not a Burmese name and is believed to have originated from early Italian travellers who compared it with their own seaside resort of Naples

Ngapali beach sunset

There are now plenty of local fish restaurants outside of the resort hotels. It is a great place to unwind and relax in the sun with very good seafood and an unspoilt beach amidst the lovely local people. It's also a great place for planning what to do next.

After relaxing at Ngapali we flew to Bagan, an ancient city not far from Mandalay. Rich with history, Bagan is a city of ancient pagodas and stupas (mound-like structures that contain Buddhist relics) where the remains of some two thousand monuments still survive.

"As rain falls equally
on the just
and the unjust,
do not burden
your heart
with judgements
but rain your kindness
equally on all."

Buddha.

Chapter 3: The Awakening

On my return to London, I could not stop thinking about our wonderful trip to Myanmar and my promise to Major to write the book about his life and the magical Lake Inle. Some months later I emailed Major arranging to see him in Yangon, (formerly Rangoon) and, knowing pretty well that his emails were censored, I knew it might take some time before I heard back. Eventually I received word in the form of the following email.

From: "major"
To: feroze
Sent: Sunday, June 2011 4:21 PM

Dear Sir,

I'm very glad and proud to hear from you that you are going to write a biography of me. If it's my life history, there will be events that the government of my country would not accept. The on coming attitude towards me will be not good. Furthermore some kind of action might be taken.

If it's a novel, then you change the names, places and events, I do hope that no misunderstanding will come between me and my government. Please be kind and forgive me, please also do understand my situation. Nevertheless, I would be waiting to read your novel. I'll supply you with any information you need.

Pardon me my late reply to you because I go to the villages there are no Internet access. During this season there are very few guests and not too busy. That's why I explore to the villages searching for some new trekking routes for the coming tour season.

May I wind up here and good luck to you.
Your loving Major."

Major had arranged the perfect cover. He would escort a renowned Singaporean monk and his entourage on a visit to a monastery at Inle. That's where we would meet.

MuMu and I arrived in Yangon on December 14 2011. It felt that much had already changed since our visit the previous year. For a start the hotel we used in the city was fully booked, which had never happened before, and a sure sign that tourism was beginning to take off. It all seemed so much busier. The endless flow of taxis in and out of this hitherto sleepy hotel was a sure indication that change was in the air. There were signs in the foyer advertising recruitment drives by foreign companies.

There was an undeniable atmosphere of optimism. Aung San Suu Kyi was preparing to take part in the forthcoming election for some 45 parliamentary seats and a thousand political prisoners had been released. President Thein Sein had already had a promising meeting with Hilary Clinton and the Myanmar papers reported a similar meeting with the European Union.

With its hard-working, literate and ethical workforce Myanmar was preparing to open its doors for business. Although China had already sneaked a large boot in through the back door.

The next day we set off for the hour long flight to He Ho and onwards for another hour or so by boat across the lake to the hotel, making sure to stock up on bird feed en route. The lake was so beautiful that I felt blessed to be making this trip once again.

On arrival we were greeted by what I can only describe as a kitchen band with staff picking up anything that came to hand – a pot or a pan – to bash out their welcome.

After a brief rest we made our way to the reception to let Major know we had arrived. I ordered some beer for us and we chatted about this and that for a while before agreeing to meet the next morning.

The lake is quite cold during the night and early morning but soon the sun was edging upwards burning off the morning mist and, with the crystal skies emerging, it was beginning to get warm. I felt good about the next chapter.

"No one saves us
but ourselves.
No one can and
no one may.
We ourselves
must walk the path."

Buddha.

Chapter 4: Fighting to Survive

Major started speaking, conscious that he was being recorded.

"My father was a Kareni and my mother a Pa'O (different ethnic tribes) and we lived in Taunggyi. We were a poor family who survived by farming vegetables and crops on some land around our small house, which was made mainly of wood and bamboo. I was one of eight children of whom only four survived to adulthood.

"My earliest recollection was from about three. As was normal, my father and my mother left me and my little brother, who was about a year old, to go to farm. My brother was strapped with a rope tied to a table so he could toddle around. There was some food left for me to eat and milk for my little brother who I had learnt to feed and look after until my parents returned home around sunset. This was my daily duty.

"I do not recall how I managed to babysit myself, let alone my little brother! One day as I rummaged around in the kitchen to fetch some milk for him I discovered a box of matches.

"I proceeded to light the matches, pretending to light the fire the way my mother did when she was home cooking. Unfortunately I did not fully appreciate that I had to blow out the matchstick when it reached the end and I let go when it became unbearably hot and it fell on the floor and began to burn the mat. In a flash the fire took hold and the dried leaves, which made up the walls of the hut, caught fire.

"I was confused and very frightened; I sensed that I had done something terribly wrong and ran out of the house as fast as possible towards the woods that lay at the foot of the drive. I sensed that the villagers were heading towards the hut but I could not look back and kept running. I felt the tears pouring from my eyes, but I kept running. I remember that it was pitch dark, there was no moonlight and I couldn't see where I was going. I kept running until I was exhausted and couldn't move any further.

"I stopped near what turned out to be a large tree and found a hollow in the magnificent trunk where I crawled in, still crying and trembling until I fell asleep. I was woken up when I heard my father shouting for me. It was dawn so he must have been looking for me all night. My parents were very relieved to have found me there the next morning and assured me that my brother was unharmed and safe and it was not my fault.

"But I still felt ashamed and vowed that I would always look after my brother and would never run away from a problem ever again.

"Our family was much loved by the villagers and, as was customary, everyone in the village pitched in and helped to reconstruct our house. Individuals contributed materials or labour or both and within a period of months the house was completed and our normal lives resumed. But now our parents took us to the farm where they could keep a close eye on our whereabouts.

"My father had been in the British Military Police (BMP). When the British left Burma in 1948 the nation became an independent republic, named the Union of Burma. Because of the oppression of minority communities the Pa'O struggle for equality began and my father like many others joined the Pa'O National Organisation (PNO) in Taunggyi, Shan State."

The Shan States were ruled by the Sawbwas (chiefs) under the British Crown during the colonial period of 1886-1948, although the Japanese occupied much of the area during the Second World War.

There were several local insurgencies after the British left in 1948. Major explained how the first Pa'O revolution had begun: "The Chiefs and their families prospered by exploiting our Pa'O people who were deprived of education and opportunities. Instead they exploited them through addiction to opium.

"As an example, when members of the Pa'O came to Taunggyi to sell their goods and produce, the tribal police encouraged them to use the many opium dens that surrounded the marketplace in return for collecting a percentage of their goods. Many became hopelessly addicted and ever more desperate.

"One day a Pa'O trader came to the Taunggyi market to sell cheroot leaves. It was not a good day for business and the trader had very few customers but at the end of the day he had to sell his goods albeit at a loss. A tribal policeman still wanted to collect his share. The trader refused to pay and a fight broke out in which the trader cut the policeman's head with his knife.

"The Pa'O man managed to escape to his village in the mountains and related this story to his people who, because of their own desperate circumstances, understood and supported him. They went from village to village to muster support against the Shan chiefs which ended in a fully-fledged armed rebellion.

"In 1949 my father joined the armed rebellion and left home for the jungle fighting a guerrilla war against these feudal rulers. During this insurgency he was part of a Pa'O group of one hundred men that sought shelter in the village of Pin Tun. They were put up with lots of different families so as not to arouse suspicion. It was there he met my mother who used to cook and look after him and the three other soldiers who were also sheltering in their house."

Major's father fell in love and asked her to marry him but she refused saying she didn't want to marry someone on the run and who was always in danger of being killed.

"But my father did not give up and asked his commanding officer to request my mother's parents to reconsider and after much lobbying her parents relented and my mother agreed to her parents' wish to marry my father."

In 1958 the Pa'O organisation agreed a truce with the government who, by that time, had done a deal with the feudal Sawbwas. When the peace process started the government began providing schooling and medical facilities in the villages. There was some progress for the Pa'O people but it was short lived.

"On March 2 1962, the military led by General Ne Win took control of Burma through a coup d'état and the oppression of the minorities by military means was re-established. On the one hand the government made some practical changes so they would win over the ordinary people; on the other hand it was eliminating opposition leaders. It did so by inviting the Pa'O leaders to come forward so the two sides could have talks; but once these individuals were identified they either never returned from the talks or subsequently disappeared.

"And so the second Pa'O uprising began and the PNO regrouped. My father, who had been working as a farmer in the intervening years, joined up again and fled to the jungle from where they organised guerrilla attacks against the Burmese armed forces (Tatmadaw).

"It was during one such encounter that my father was killed. My mother was left with eight children including two sets of twins.

"When the Pa'O leadership started re-mobilising its troops for the second insurgence, my mother had pleaded with my father not to join. But he felt it was his duty and so he paid the ultimate price. He was one of the first to die in a government attack on their jungle base. I was six years old at that time.

"No one in his unit was prepared to break the news to his family and it was almost a year before my mother was told. "He had left my mother without any means of support. Both sets of twins later died from malaria. There were no mosquito nets and people drank unpurified water at that time. There were no medical facilities. The situation for the Pa'O people was desperate."I am not sure how the rest of us managed to survive.

"My mother is still alive at the age of seventy three. She married three more times but could not find any other husband who could replace my father. She is now single and living with one of my brothers.

"As soon as the second uprising began the government closed the schools and hospitals in retaliation. I was six, fatherless, with no real prospect of any further education and was now facing an uncertain future.

"I was very grateful to my uncle who took me into his family and sent me to the primary school at Inle."

"I find hope in
the darkest of days,
and focus in
the brightest.
I do not judge
the universe."

Dalai Lama

Chapter 5: Lessons Learned

When Major was nine he was sent to his next school as a boarder. His ability to court controversy was never far away.

This was at the time when the Pa'O had made a short-lived peace following the first insurgency. The government had responded by opening a few schools, including the one attended by the young Major.

The children all slept in a neat row of double bunk beds. They followed a strict code of cleanliness and discipline in the army tradition. There was only one form of punishment and it was used often – caning. The only thing that varied was the number of lashes depending on the seriousness of the offence. This was zero tolerance, but the children accepted it as completely fair.

The school existed on a strict understanding that the headmaster was always right and the boys always did exactly what they were told. So when it was discovered that someone had left a turd by one the children's beds, all hell broke loose. The boys conducted their own investigation rather than inform the headmaster, rightly fearing that to do so would result in one thing. The toilets were some distance from the dormitories so whoever was responsible must have deliberately placed it there. But no one was prepared to own up.

The next morning the same thing happened. And again the following day. There was clearly a serial prankster at work. Each time it happened the boys removed the offending matter before the headmaster could discover it.

But attempts to uncover the culprit were getting nowhere and if he didn't own up the whole school faced a caning. Major decided to take matters into his own hands. He would tell the head what was going on unless whoever was responsible owned up. So the next morning on discovering yet another deposit Major kept his word and reported the matter to the head.

As expected the headmaster asked the children if the culprit was prepared to own up rather than cause trouble for his fellow students. The children closed ranks; no one owned up to the offence.

The headmaster asked all the boys to line up and drop their pants so he could conduct an inspection. In this rather crude but effective way the culprit was eventually identified, a model student called Khin Maung. He was the most unlikely of people to stoop to such a thing.

Asked for an explanation, the boy came clean and blurted out how he had been too frightened to go to the toilets because they were under the banyan tree which villagers had told him was haunted by a demon who craved the blood of young boys.

Flushed with his success the headmaster was already tapping his cane on the palm of his hand in anticipation; warming up in readiness. His quivering student was resigned to his fate. But instead the headmaster had a much better idea.

"Khin Maung," he said, "I will break from the traditional punishment. Instead you will spend the whole night alone under the banyan tree." Khin Maung took his punishment like a man and survived without the loss of a single drop of blood. He was both cured of his antics and his superstition.

Major's school days were cut short by the second Pa'O revolution that resulted in the government withdrawing its funding programme for education. There was then no money for the teachers' pay or for the upkeep of the school which rapidly fell into serious disrepair. Eventually only the headmaster remained. There was hardly any food and the boys became desperate – but they weren't the only ones in search of something to eat.

As the walls surrounding the school began to collapse, it became common practice for everyone and everything to simply wander through the school. One such trespasser was the local cow that regularly visited the school kitchen in a determined search for food. Often the cow was unsuccessful  but such encounters resulted in significant collateral damage as it barged its way around smashing crockery and fittings, which the boys then had to clean up.

Major hatched a cunning plot with the boys to capture the cow. This would not only stop the trespass but also provide much needed meat for the boys who had to survive much of the time on a diet of boiled rice donated by villagers.

One evening when the headmaster was away visiting his family the scene was set for the ambush.

As the cow entered the building the older boys put a noose around the cow's head and tied it to the tree outside to stop it running away. Having secured the animal, Major carried out the swift coup de grace. The younger boys had already lit the fire outside and soon the barbecue was glowing. A feast indeed. Or was it the last supper?

The next day the cow's owner came to the school looking for his animal only to discover evidence that it had been slaughtered. The headmaster was forced to pay up and that exhausted the last of the school's funds. The school closed.

The second Pa'O insurgency had started with a vengeance. The government had abruptly cut off the financial lifeline for the school and once again the children were abandoned.

Major was twelve when he was handed over to a monastery as a helper to one of the monks. Whilst this was supposed to form a part of the young Major's religious education there was always time for other adventures.

Major's main job, other than as a general helper to his assigned monk, was to accompany him from house to house collecting food. Since monks are only permitted to do this and to eat between dawn and midday, this generally meant an early start. A monk's helper isn't bound by these rules so Major readily received and accepted money and other fringe benefits. It proved a lucrative way of supplementing his meagre rations and possessions. His formal religious education was confined to a few hours in the evening.

Aside from these duties Major and his fellow helpers cooked and looked after themselves. It was a well-ordered and harmonious existence until...

One day there was a commotion in the village. Apparently the local BCP (Burma Communist Party) had been raided by the military police. They were attempting to recapture a BCP activist who had managed to escape after being wounded in crossfire.

Later that night Major heard whimpering, like a wild animal in pain. He went out with the intention of rescuing it but when he opened the door of an outhouse he found a man covered in blood and lying unconscious on the floor. Major quickly dressed his wound with strips of bandage he made from his shirt and then alerted the monks.

It transpired that the man, whose name was Ti Hha, had been shot in the shoulder and had lost a lot of blood. Thanks to Major's rapid intervention he was at least still alive; but he would need urgent medical attention. Major pleaded with the monks to give him sanctuary and promised he would personally tend to him. The monks reluctantly agreed to take the man in even though they realised he was a wanted terrorist. As a wanted man there was no way Ti Hha could be taken to hospital. Ti Hha stayed at the monastery with Major taking on the role of chief nurse. Without specialist hospital treatment it was touch and go, but after several weeks the man recovered.

On sitting up in bed, the first thing he asked Major to do was to fetch some rice wine. Fortunately Ti Hha had some money and so that evening Major managed to buy enough wine to not only intoxicate Ti Hha but also half a dozen of the monks' other young helpers. The monastery was briefly transformed into a club as they drank and laughed the night away.

Now fourteen, this was Major's introduction to both alcohol and a hangover. His education was coming on in leaps and bounds! Under Ti Hha's tutelage on most nights when the monks were asleep, Major would accompany him on his drinking and womanising sessions. But Major was a lightweight and couldn't manage to burn the candle at both ends, which meant he kept falling asleep in lessons.

Inevitably it wasn't long before Ti Hha was exposed and banished from the monastery forever. But along the way, Major had become a man.

"My Pa'O village was not far from Inle, in the mountains surrounding the lake, so I was able to get home from time to time," said Major. "After I completed primary school I went to live in Taunggyi.

"My uncle worked as a driver for a local business and that kept him away from home for long periods of time. He could just about afford for me to live with him. But I had to earn my keep. My aunt came from a very rich family and refused to live as a peasant. Indeed when her first child was born she refused to breast feed and demanded a wet nurse at the hospital!

"But I had been brought up in the countryside so I knew how to cope and made myself indispensable. I got up every day at four; cooked breakfast for the family and after school cleaned the house and cooked dinner for the children as well as my aunt. I became the resident nanny, housekeeper and man about the house as well as an occasional student.

"When I was fifteen or so I managed get a job at the local golf course as a caddy. I found the time to caddy at least once every evening and managed two rounds on Saturdays and Sundays. My fortunes changed – I would earn as much as a thousand kyats per month ($1) – no paltry sum in those days, and the money helped start my college fund.

"However, as I grew older I began to feel uncomfortable being a caddy, which was a job associated with children. So instead I got a job in Taunggyi working for a rich merchant as an odd job man, gardener and troubleshooter.

"I managed to pass my matriculation exams when I was nineteen. I was still living with my uncle then. I had a six month gap before starting college and although I had saved some money from my caddying days and working for the merchant, it still wasn't enough to see me through this next stage of my education. I needed to find something to bridge the gap."

Major's life was about to change again.

Education is what
remains after one
has forgotten what one
has learned in school.

Albert Einstein

Chapter 6: Deadly Dealings

The next chapter in Major's life was to involve some of his most adventurous and dangerous exploits in his life and would shape a future where he would become a wanted man.

"I knew I had to make much more money to see me through my first year in college and I realised that the amount I could earn in the six months I had before starting was never going to be enough. I had to find something or some way of making a fast buck.

"The opportunity came when one day I was buying some vegetables in the market and I overheard a man buying cattle to take to Thailand. I was curious and when I approached and talked to him it transpired that not only did he want to buy more cattle but he was also recruiting strong young men who would help him take them across the hills and through the jungles and rivers from Taunggyi into Thailand by smuggling them across the Burmese border at Mae Hong Son.

"We struck a deal and in the next few weeks I helped him to recruit a group of thirty or so young men and to buy one hundred and fifty head of cattle from various markets around He Ho and Taunggyi.

"The dealer, he was called Ne Tin, had raised the money by selling his farm and borrowing money from friends and relatives. It was a perilous but potentially lucrative venture. Success would bring relative riches – but failure would have devastating consequences.

"We would start our journey in the evening from the outskirts of Se Sang (near Taunggyi) avoiding the town itself. We had to travel light as the round trip could last anything between two and five weeks depending on the weather and the level of security en route.

"Our rations were made up of uncooked rice and dry spices with salt and chillies all rolled up in a cloth, which resembled a long sausage. We carried it over our shoulders like a bag. We also took a kidney-shaped US army pot, which served as a cooking pan as well as a plate with different compartments for rice and spices. Last, but not least, a plastic sheet, which had multiple uses. Laid on the ground it became a place to sleep; worn over us, a raincoat; and when cleaned, a table cloth and a plate all rolled into one. We also carried rope, a knife and matches.

"We walked throughout the first night until we reached the Phon River. Although there was a bridge crossing, it was always heavily patrolled by soldiers. So we had to find a safe crossing point where the river narrowed. We used a spot where the river was no more than fifteen metres wide. As a lot of the men couldn't swim we tied a rope from a tree on one bank to a tree on the other side of the river so the men could walk across holding the rope and not be swept away by the strong currents. The cows were able to swim across quite comfortably. The river was usually no more than waist high at this point.

"We had to adapt according to the conditions at that time of year. In summer it was usually very dry and often we couldn't find fresh water. This meant we had to compete with the cows to drink the remnants of small pools of stagnant water left over from the rains. This was a breeding ground for mosquitoes and the men often suffered from malaria and water-borne diseases but there was no choice but to take the gamble, or die of thirst or risk dying from malaria.

"When you are dehydrated and suffering from intense heat and thirst, the choice becomes a lot easier.

"During the monsoons when heavy rains made it impossible to find anywhere dry enough to cook our rice or to sleep, it often meant wrapping the plastic sheet around you and crouching under a tree to try and get a little rest until the morning came and we were able to move on.

"Not only did we have to contend with the hazards of travel through difficult terrain and weather conditions, we also had to avoid the government troops and a hive of other minority separatist parties: the BCP (Burmese Communist Party), the WNA (Wa National Army) and KNPP (Karenni National Progressive Party). They were all fleeing from persecution and constantly fighting government forces, or indeed each other. They competed to collect taxes or smuggle opium to fund their insurgent activities.

"All these tribes expected payment in return for safe passage so we did everything to avoid them. When we did bump into them the going rate was usually 5000 kyats ($5) per cow. The WNA members were very organised and controlled the Salween, the main river that needed to be crossed. As far as we were concerned, at least they provided a service by allowing us to use their canoes – albeit for an extortionate price!

"The Salween River crossing was the most difficult part of our journey and often the raging currents meant the crossing was particularly dangerous. This was the ultimate challenge and in the rainy season the water was extremely deep and often very rough. It was not possible to cross by wading or swimming.

"So we would resort to having to hire boats from the WNA. Each man sat in the boat with a cow submerged in the water next to him. To stop the cow from panicking and being swept away in the currents we would hold the cow's head in our arms to give it comfort. It was the custom for cows to have holes pierced through their nostrils; we'd pass a rope through it and this would help to control them.

"We'd then tie the cow to the boat. The key was to make sure that the animal felt secure and didn't panic and overturn the boat. The looks of terror in the large longing eyes of the cows as they clung desperately to the boats will remain with me forever.

"Typically there would be five men in each boat sitting in a line one behind the other with five cows correspondingly lined up submerged in the water. This meant making several crossings over two or three days to ensure that all the cattle got safely to the other side. There were several mishaps and one fatality when one of my friends was swept overboard and drowned while trying to control a panic-stricken cow. The current was so strong that he was never seen again.

"But probably the most difficult part of the journey was avoiding the Burmese regular army troops who were constantly on the lookout for insurgents and often engaged in fierce gun battles with them. We did everything to avoid them, always making sure that there was an advance party of a few of our boys several miles ahead of the herd.

However on one such journey the army followed the cattle footprints and were able to quickly catch up with us and our slow moving herd. We had no choice but to abandon our livestock. The consequences of being caught didn't bear thinking about.

"In the following months we made several successful journeys. Against the backdrop of the system that operated at the time there was no room, and certainly no money, in running a legitimate business. Instead it became the norm to smuggle our comparatively cheap goods, especially cattle, across the border to more lucrative markets in Thailand.

"Indeed it became a way of life in border villages so that even housewives would dodge the border guards to sell their fruit and vegetables at many times the price they would fetch if sold locally at the fixed low price. This became our economic way of life."

"When you realise
how perfect
everything is
you will tilt
your head back
and laugh at the sky."

Buddha.

Chapter 7: Voyage of Discovery

Major had arranged for a four wheel drive to take us from Inle across the mountains to the surrounding Pa'O villages and onwards towards Taunggyi where MuMu wanted to meet up with her cousins for the first time on this trip. Virtually the whole fifty miles or so of the journey was on dirt roads that would have been impossible in an ordinary car. The driver (who used to be a truck driver for the Pa'O) was in his element in this terrain negotiating the deeply rutted and muddy tracks that linked the villages.

There were several detours to, as Major put it: "avoid any awkward situations." By which he meant any encounters with military patrols. The landscape was lush with forests and in between crops seemed to have been planted everywhere.

We could see people bathing and washing clothes in the many streams. The Pa'O are distinctive because they mostly dress in black, this is based on their belief that they are descendants of Nagah (a mythical dragon). They also wear their clothes layered like the scales of a dragon. In contrast they wear colourful headgear. We could see many examples of this in the men and women who were working side by side in the fields.

Our first stop was the village of Pin Tonn before travelling north through Saung Phoe, Naung Ya Sai and on to Taunggyi.

Major stopped at a few huts along the way to visit families and check up on the progress of the welfare work he had been carrying out in the area – helping to find work for young people at the hotel or helping to provide funds for their education. He was clearly still deeply involved in fighting their corner though now in a peaceful way. He was obviously well known and hugely respected.

We finally reached Major's village and stopped at a cottage. We were invited to sit around the fireplace where we were served green tea blended with roasted sesame seeds, which gave it a lovely flavour and which reflected the family's warm smiles.

The grandmother shook hands and was amazed how soft my hands were. She beckoned the rest of the family to scrutinise them – each had to have a feel and discuss them before I was given a nod of approval and allowed to sit down.

There were no modern amenities in the village. No electricity, TV or landline telephones. We were expected to remove our shoes before entering the cottage. There was just one large communal room, which served as a living room and kitchen by day and bedroom by night. There were no beds and I guessed they simply slept on the rush floors.

Interestingly there were no animals of any sort in the village, either pets or livestock. Instead they bought their meat from local markets. It may have had something to do with their attitude to cleanliness.

Major explained how the government had built a new hospital in the area but that it was practically empty. To ensure it wasn't closed down due to the lack of patients, the villagers made sure they turned up pretending to be ill before any inspection!

The Pa'O are a handsome and dignified people who possess a sense of serenity which is etched in their genial faces; expressions that we in a world of plenty seem to have lost.

There was always so much to explore, both the way of life and the country itself. Having now experienced some of the mountainous areas we wanted to venture into other uncharted waters, and travel to the south side of the lake. This involved a three hour boat journey through the long channel that linked Lake Inle with Lake Samkar.

After an hour or so we stopped to visit the market at Mawbe. As we approached we were greeted by a flotilla of small boats filled with pretty smiling girls armed with trinkets and knick-knacks all eager to try and catch us before we landed. Again, there was no hard sell. The girls were happy and laughing and if we chose to buy they were over the moon – if not, they still smiled. In many ways their presence felt more like a reception committee than a sales pitch.

Markets are a key part of the local trading tradition and boats of all shapes and sizes jostle for space around the crowded landing areas.

Our boatman tried to get us as close as possible, but in the end the only way to reach the shore was by hopping from boat to boat.

This was where members of the Intha tribe would bring their fish and vegetables to barter or sell in exchange for grain and meat from the Pa'O people. There were a few stalls selling trinkets for tourists but this was mainly a market for locals. We stayed a short while, took some pictures, drank some green tea and then set off again on our journey south.

After a few minutes we reached Mawbe Bridge. We were stopped by some uniformed troops who were stationed on the bridge overhead. One of them lowered a basket to us on a rope and Major put some money into it.

A few words were exchanged with the senior officer via the walkie-talkie that Major was carrying. There was obviously some sort of established understanding between Major and the soldiers and without further delay we were allowed to continue. After another hour or so we stopped again – this time at Samkar with its enchanting and haunting ruined stupas – many of which had trees growing through them.

Opposite there was an altogether different attraction: an illicit brewery. Here they produced various lethal concoctions using the staple ingredient – rice!

It would have been impolite to refuse to sample a drop or two, and having done so we headed for home, stopping for a sumptuous local feast on the way and arriving at Inle late in that evening exhausted but exhilarated.

The sinking stupas of Samkar

The next day Major had to leave unexpectedly, apparently for an emergency meeting with the Pa'O. Our journey was again put on hold. But we knew we'd be back.

"There has to
be evil so that
good can prove
its purity above it."

Buddha.

Chapter 8: The Winds of Change

As we prepared for our third trip to Myanmar the world's front pages were plastered with the pictures of President Obama embracing Aung San Suu Kyi who was freed in 2010 after years of house arrest. The US President spoke of rewarding the regime by opening up trade links but also stressed the importance of embracing the various minority communities within Myanmar – a reference to the most recent violence between Buddhists and Muslims in the State of Rakhine.

Myanmar continued to struggle to come to terms with democracy. President Thein Sein – who had been the prime minister in the previous administration with the rank of General – is considered a moderate and a reformist and, since taking over at the country's helm, he's allowed Aung San Suu Kyi to resume her political activities.

But while there's been undoubted progress, corruption remains rife in Myanmar and many people have also been quick to cash in on the decision to open the country's borders to mass tourism.

Cousin Mazhar, who was the general manager of a hotel in Yangon, told us about a European journalist who had pre-booked a hotel room in the city for $75 a night but some days before his arrival he was told the rate had doubled. He had reluctantly accepted only to be then told it had gone up to $225! At that point he wisely opted to go elsewhere.

There were also stories circulating about how certain monasteries required significant 'donations' before they would bless and approve business licenses. Many of these transactions were apparently being negotiated over a round of golf.

So much seemed to be changing. We wondered if the country was losing its innocence.

After an eighteen hour flight from London we touched down in Yangon. We stayed the first night in the city before catching the early flight on the following morning to He Ho where Ting and his sister May Mae picked us up at the airport. Ting had borrowed a jeep so we were able to use the rougher road, which meant a much shorter journey by boat to the hotel.

It seemed my love of wine had preceded me because Ting immediately presented me with a bottle of French Bordeaux he'd managed to buy in Taunggyi, which must have cost him an arm and a leg. This was served at our customary special 'late' lunch that Ting had organised on the terrace of the hotel.

Major was waiting to greet us and introduced us to someone he referred to as: 'our leader'. I had brought two bottles of Major's favourite Scotch at the duty free shop at Heathrow, which I knew would be a good way to loosen tongues. At least I hoped it would.

The lake looked beautiful in the dying moments of the setting sun. But Ting explained that the lake was getting smaller because of encroaching vegetation which was beginning to spread across the surface as a result of the intensive use of fertilizers and a growing dependence on the lake for irrigation.

The next day we resumed our meeting at Major's usual table outside. Although it was almost a year since we'd last sat here it seemed like only yesterday.

"I do not believe in a fate
that falls on men
however they act;
but I do believe
in a fate that falls
on them
unless they act."

Buddha

Chapter 9: Dangerous Liaisons

By this time Major had saved up enough money from smuggling to enrol into Mandalay University as a maths student. He continued to make three or four trips a year smuggling livestock into Thailand using a by now well-rehearsed route.

This involved trekking from Taunggyi south east towards Hsi Hseng then crossing the Nampon and Salween rivers to the Thai border near Mae Hong Son – a round trip which took several weeks. These 'business' trips had graduated from small scale adventures – albeit risky ones – to becoming a thriving export and import operation. Cattle were traded for luxury goods in Thailand, which were then supplied to the shopkeepers in Taunggyi.

His movements were well known by those manning the Pa'O checkpoints and Major made sure he kept them sweet by always bringing them some presents and spending time drinking and smoking with them. But one day their attitude changed.

He was politely detained and taken to see the local commanding officer. The CO was clearly aware of Major's talent of being able to move goods seamlessly through a string of villages past a number of army checkpoints and across the border without being detected. Quite a feat. He had managed it by enrolling a network of tribal helpers who were charmed by his personality and generosity and who remained loyal to a man. Major had established a secure highway from Taunggyi to Mae Hong Son, which the Pa'O now wished to exploit.

Major's already risky lifestyle was about to become a whole lot more perilous.

The Pa'O wanted Major to become a secret agent. His role would be to indoctrinate and recruit fellow students at Mandalay University to the Pa'O insurgency.

Back at Mandalay University, Major set up an office and a Pa'O faculty that ostensibly dealt with cultural issues, but which actually acted as a front for the Pa'O cause for which he campaigned tirelessly. He also distributed the Pa'O newsletter on the campus, which was published and printed at their camp HQ deep in the jungle on a dilapidated manually operated printing machine. None of this was illegal in the sense that he was simply promoting a greater understanding of the culture and history associated with an established tribal people.

But behind the scenes there was a hidden agenda. Major was carrying out his orders to mobilise young recruits for the Pa'O army which desperately needed new recruits in the face of an ever more aggressive Burmese military presence.

Such activity could be interpreted as terrorism and Major needed to be both alert and smart.

Young Pa'O students who'd signed up to the faculty because of the initial soft sell were invited to secret meetings and fed a more aggressive sales pitch with an altogether different agenda. At these meetings Major served up a lethal mixture of alcohol and propaganda. It did the trick. He quickly established a solid following of students eager to join forces with the rebels.

They were deployed in a variety of roles, some in support and some in training camps to become fighters. Major set up a lasting infrastructure at the university which continued to indoctrinate Pa'O students for years to come. He had also found a safe house when needed.

After graduating and successfully setting up a self-sustaining Pa'O recruitment office there, he was summoned to the Pa'O command HQ in the jungle.

Among the high-ranking officers he met was Bo Kyaw who at the time was the organisation's Chief Funding Officer (CFO). Bo was to provide the resources for Major's operations and from then on the two of them worked closely together.

It wasn't long before he was promoted to a new role – to set up and formalise an intelligence unit including organising the safe passage of recruits and personnel to and from Pa'O areas. This was a new non-combatant position and after some negotiation it was agreed that the position was to bear the rank of Major.

The Pa'O had recently reached an agreement for the KNU (Karen National Union) to provide military training to their recruits. The KNU were the best trained and the second largest of the minority groups. Being Christians they had joined forces with the British during World War Two and had been well trained by them. In return for their support the British had promised them a separate state, but history was to tell another story.

Major's first task was to arrange safe passage for the first fifty recruits from the Taunggyi area to the training camp which was close to the border with Thailand about two hundred miles away in the state of Kayin – much of it through difficult and dangerous terrain.

But even before the journey could begin Major faced a unique challenge as a spy master – to kit out the recruits with Pa'O uniforms that didn't actually exist!

Having realised it would be unwise to march his new troops to the nearest tailor in Taunggyi, Major adopted a more subtle approach. He selected soldiers of different sizes and shapes and, armed with rolls of suitable green curtain material, sent them off to a variety of tailors in the area.

The finishing touches, including the Pa'O army markings, were added back at the Pa'O warehouse in Taunggyi – a shack at the back of a friend's farmhouse.

Now fully booted and suited, Major and his recruits headed off in a convoy of jeeps through Kaya territory to Loikaw. This part of the journey was reasonably easy along a well-trodden path for Major and amongst friendly people.

As they left Loikaw a villager warned them that government troops had been stationed in the next town. There was no way round the town and Major had to find a solution. He had no idea how long the soldiers would remain there. Time was of the essence.

As they waited Major spotted a Christian funeral procession entering the town. He asked the pastor, whom he had met before, if he would allow his men to join in. The pastor agreed and the men entered the town without being challenged. Arrangements had already been made to house them in return for a donation to church funds, as well as to the village chief!

Up to four men were billeted in each house but because they didn't speak the Kaya language (though Major did) and the villagers didn't speak Pa'O,

Major felt it best to keep social interaction to a minimum. The solution lay in providing the men with plenty of alcohol, which worked a treat. They slept for a whole day until it was dark and the government forces had left.

But they were far from being out of danger. The rest of the journey meant negotiating deep jungle and traversing dangerous terrain. Major made sure they avoided any confrontation with the many other tribes and drug gangs that operated along the way. This often meant waving a white flag and negotiating a bribe.

In this way Major and his troops made their way safely through the Kaya state and onwards through the south east to Mae Hong Son in Thailand. There they were escorted further south along the border towards Mae Sariang and on to their final destination, the training camp at Minaplaw. He was to make several more of these hazardous trips.

In order to create an alias for Major, the Pa'O arranged for him to take up a post as a schoolteacher at the monastery in Inle. After a few months the Pa'O arranged for an individual of similar age and looks to replace him. It was a clever ruse. To those who knew nothing of this ploy, Major now existed as a school teacher. This duplicity allowed him to move around from village to village carrying out his clandestine activities. Now and again he would appear at the monastery to re-establish his credentials.

Much of Major's work involved moving men and supplies through the urban areas to the jungle training camps, but he was also busy gathering vital information about the activities and whereabouts of government forces.

There was one particular assignment he remembers well. It involved tracking down a missing Pa'O commander who had been captured by government forces in an ambush on one of their camps near Inle. Commander Aung Tin Oo held far too much information about the Pa'O command structure and identities of undercover operatives for comfort. The military police were well versed in torture techniques which some of their officers had learnt whilst fighting with the Japanese against the British in the Second World War. It was only a matter of time before they would break Aung Tin either by threats to him or his family.

So much was at stake that Major was personally assigned to track him down and find a way to either spring him or silence him.

Because Major and the Pa'O enjoyed such local support it was easy enough to discover what the government troops had been up to and if they were still holding Aung Tin in one of the surrounding villages. If that was the case there was a good chance of finding him. The fear was that he had been moved to a military base in one of the cities. Major had little influence outside the Shan and Kaya areas.

Word soon came through that Aung Tin was being held captive at a military camp in one of the Kaya villages that Major was very familiar with as it was on the way to the Pa'O training camp. The village was about twenty-five miles away by jeep. The journey was extremely difficult because he had to travel at night along rough dirt roads avoiding the regular military checkpoints. Eventually he had to abandon the jeep and make his way for the last five miles on foot. This journey had taken all night and by the time Major arrived at the village it was getting light.

On the hilltop overlooking the village he could see the army garrison's makeshift camp in the village school and the surrounding compound. There were some two hundred or so soldiers camped outside and he guessed probably about another hundred in the school buildings – far too many to risk a Pa'O assault. Besides, the military troops were much better equipped than the Pa'O and so fighting their way in wasn't an option.

Major carefully made his way into the village. As he spoke Karenni and knew a lot of people there, he didn't look out of place in the early morning activity of village life. But he still needed to find a way into the camp. He had to get closer to the school building.

That evening he made his way to one of the drinking establishments near the army camp. He knew the bar owner so Major bribed him to serve the strongest drink he possessed in the largest measures. He wanted to ensure that it was 'happy hour' all night so that tongues were well oiled enough for him to work the bar for information.

The evening dragged by. He picked up some useful general information about troop numbers, their routine and the way they were supplied, but Major didn't find out anything that was going to help him get into the place. It seemed the villagers got on pretty well with their enforced guests. The only tension came when off-duty soldiers got drunk and loud and picked arguments with the locals.

There were rumours that this unit had uncovered the location of the Pa'O training camp and was preparing for an assault. But since the officers remained largely confined to barracks this was all based on gossip from the lower ranks and was therefore pretty unreliable as far as Major was concerned.

He was so desperate for a breakthrough that he prayed for inspiration.

It was Kason, the second month in the Myanmar calendar which falls between April and May. This is one of the most sacred periods for Buddhists. It is the month of Buddha's birth as well as the month when he attained enlightenment whilst meditating under a Bodhi tree. It's also when he died. The festival to celebrate this nationally and most revered of occasions takes place on the full moon and involves pouring clean and cool water on the Bodhi Tree as a symbol of veneration to the Buddha.

Major realised that the only people who could gain unfettered – indeed welcome – access to the army barracks would be the monks when they entered as part of their procession. If he could find a way to join their procession it would also give him access to the school compound which was home to one of the oldest Bodhi trees in the village.

So he made his way to the monastery without any real idea how he would persuade the monks to play along with the deception. As he walked into the monastery he found the monks were involved in their preparation for the festival. Standing and smiling in front of him was someone Major instantly recognised – it was Ti Hha, the Communist Party escapee who the monks had given refuge to all those years ago. But hadn't he been expelled from the monastery? It transpired that Ti Hha had repented and joined this monastery some years later as a novice monk and here he was now a fully-fledged monk!

Although now a monk he still possessed his revolutionary spirit and readily agreed to help Major. He remembered how the young Major had saved his life and tended to him all those years ago. This was at great risk to the monastery's reputation as monks were forbidden from direct political involvement. But Ti Hha was determined to repay Major's kindness.

98

He gave Major one of his saffron robes and helped him shave his head. Ti Hha introduced Major to his colleagues as a monk who was visiting from the monastery in Inle. Major was already familiar with the protocol of monastic life having served as a monk's helper all those years ago, so fitting in with the routine for the next three days until the festival started was pretty straightforward.

The bigger problem was finding a way of concealing his revolver while dressed as a monk. But he had an idea. He took one of the monk's alms bowls and created a false bottom large enough to hide his ex British army .38 Smith and Wesson. He covered the revolver in a plastic bag so it was waterproof and placed it in the false bottom of the bowl.

Major now had half a plan that would get him into the army camp with his weapon, but then what?

On the day of the festival the monks' procession started with the usual chanting in praise of Buddha with the villagers lining the street or joining in the parade. The monks prayed out loud as the followers stopped to pour water onto the Bodhi trees as they went by.

Finally, the procession reached the barracks where the camp commander welcomed them into the school compound. On this occasion the public wasn't allowed to enter. The procession reached the Bodhi tree that stood by the side of the school building and the monks began their prayers and blessings with all the soldiers joining in. While they were distracted Major slipped away unnoticed. He had spotted Aung Tin peering through a window of the school building and so Major began making his way along the corridor in that direction.

As expected, the room was guarded. Major was surprised to see only two soldiers, the others having probably left to join the ceremony. He moved towards the soldiers putting his hand in the alms bowl and sprinkling water on them. Slightly taken aback, but overawed, they bowed to Major in reverence. He blessed them and moved towards the cell door.

The upper part of the door had been removed and fitted with steel bars so that the guards could keep an eye on their prisoner. Major looked Aung Tin straight in the eye, silently willing him not to show any recognition. After sprinkling some water on the prisoner, Aung Tin asked if he could have a drink from the bowl. The guards, still feeling a sense of privileged elation, agreed and opened the top part of the cell door. Major handed him the bowl: "Drink from the bowl every day and you will see the light."

He turned, blessed the soldiers once more, and began to make his way back outside where he rejoined the throng of people. The next day there was a huge commotion in camp and sounds of gunfire.

Nothing further was heard of Aung Tin Oo.

"All things appear
and disappear
because of the
concurrence of causes
and conditions.
Nothing ever exists
entirely alone;
everything is
in relation
to everything else."

Buddha.

Chapter 10: Love Lies Bleeding

In many developing countries boys are looked on by their parents as wage earners and insurance for when they're old. They're seen as better investments because they go out to work whereas girls tend to marry which costs their parents money in the form of a dowry. So girls are often seen as a liability and boys an asset as far as the family's balance sheet is concerned.

The position in Myanmar is radically different in that boys and girls are brought up side by side in school and work shoulder to shoulder in the fields and in offices. Girls are as likely to look after their parents as boys. This has a lot to do with the Buddhist teaching of mutual respect.

However when it comes to love, boys are expected to make the first practical move. This, in most cases, involves what we in the West would see as an incredibly old-fashioned form of courtship. The suitor carries a set of handwritten letters in readiness for meeting someone he fancies.

The choice of letter depends on the stage the relationship is at. In the early stages the letter might simply ask: "I like you very much. Do you like me?" Later the letter might recite some poetry or profess undying love. The boy has to take a bit of a gamble on the content. Be too timid and risk instant rejection. Too bold and a slap!

Major, needless to say, had his own version of events.

"Much of the time I had been moving around from place to place so I never had any chance to build a relationship." He had tried the traditional love letter route without any real success and had eventually decided he needed a different strategy. In desperation he approached one of his colleagues who had a reputation for producing successful love letters. They even came with a guarantee – but at a price based on a no win–no fee basis.

Armed with the letters and renewed confidence Major tried his luck but met with only minor success. Although they didn't bring him much luck, he decided to pay up rather than own up to his failure.

However, he had his sights firmly fixed on someone special all along; let's call her Thae' Mar for the sake of anonymity. What happened depends on whether you believe Major or Thae' Mar's version of events.

Thae' Mar tells it like this: "I was a young student nurse and, to make extra money, worked in a general store in Taunggyi. We had this rather strange customer (Major) who would come into the shop up to ten times a day to buy one item at a time. This aroused my curiosity. He was very mysterious and nobody knew what he actually did and he would disappear for long periods of time. He never handed me a love letter so I had no idea if he was really interested.

"My next encounter was when he was discreetly wheeled into the hospital where I was then working with a suspected gall bladder complication requiring surgery. But, although I was a mere trainee nurse, it didn't take me long to figure out that he had in fact been shot in the stomach. The hospital had to falsify their records so that Major wasn't discovered. I tended to him and he made a full recovery."
But did he?

Thae' Mar continued: "He kept coming back time and again to the hospital, not for his stomach wound but for a problem with his heart!"

Thae' Mar finally succumbed and they agreed they would marry once Major finished university and she had completed her training as a nurse.

They remain married to this day.

End of Part One

"I never see
what has been done.
I only see what remains
to be done."

Buddha.

Part Two

Chapter 11:
The Day My Life Changed

Having exhausted all the tourist attractions on the lake we asked Major if we could venture even further south beyond Samkar and the clandestine brewery.

Major pondered for a while. "Tourists are not permitted to go much beyond Samkar as the government cannot guarantee their safety," he said.

It seemed much of the area was under the quasi-control of local militia and there had been a spate of foreigners being robbed. Apparently some Japanese tourists had recently been kidnapped and held for ransom.
But Major then added: "I will see what can be arranged."

A few hours later and we were told we could leave for Lwe Paw early the next morning.

Lwe Paw was between four and five hours south by boat depending on the conditions. The route meant crossing the main lake then going through the long narrow channel under Mawbe Bridge before entering a wider lake near Samkar. Then it was south through another channel to our planned destination. What could go wrong?

We set out very early the next morning after some strong hot coffee. The local coffee produced at Lake Inle is amazing and can give any fancy blend a run for its money. It was a winter's morning. Temperatures can drop close to zero at night but during the day the sun can burn you if you forgo the protection of sun cream or an umbrella. Between these extremes the morning mist lies over the lake like a soft white feather duvet. It can take up to two hours for the sun to burn off the mist and shine through in its brilliance.

Major had arranged for blankets, windbreakers and umbrellas which proved invaluable on the choppy waters of the big lake near Samkar. Umbrellas are truly multipurpose. They protect you from the monsoon rain, the sun during the midday heat, and – if held out horizontally – keep you dry from the spray. Major insisted we wear life-jackets at all times on this trip as visibility was especially poor when we set out and the surface was particularly rough near Samkar.

To begin with it seemed like the boat was gliding on a bed of clouds. There was no sign of the water – just a distant horizon above the low-lying mist.

Major stood at the helm in his camouflage cap giving instructions about our course to the boatman at the stern, who seemed to react to every one of his hand signals. This was satnav technology Myanmar style!

The lake begins to come alive at sunrise. On our way we passed lots of small boats each with two or three children rowing to school, their neat school uniforms, comprising white shirts with dark shorts or longyis, glistening in the sun.

We could also see the fishermen laying out their nets and the general hustle and bustle on the lake accompanied by the mellow chanting from the local monastery. The scene was picture perfect with its own soundtrack.

After about an hour or so of navigating through rampant weed and other obstacles we reached Mawbe Bridge. There were some basic toilet facilities there so we were able to take a comfort break. The bridge itself was patrolled by militia guards stationed at either end. Major walked towards the sentries who clearly recognised him and appeared to greet him like an old friend, though we were too far away to hear what was being said. Soon Major returned accompanied by someone associated with the militia but who wasn't wearing a uniform.

Children going to school

He quietly took up position in the stern of the boat which we assumed was to ensure our continued safety and to help negotiate our way past other militia posts. Apparently these were the very same soldiers who fought with the PNO guerrillas during the insurgency, some of whom had served under Major's command. Now they formed part of the quasi-government local security force for that area.

We reached Samkar after three hours or so and Major stopped at a cottage with a huge veranda that stood in the middle of the lake. This was the final staging post and watering hole for most adventure seeking tourists and as far as we would normally have been allowed to go.

We moored and went into the cottage. Major ordered green tea and some snacks but the main purpose was to choose the menu for lunch on our return. This way the ladies who owned the restaurant had time to paddle across into town to buy fresh ingredients which would be served with the local rice wine as an optional extra. They call it wine, but at 40% proof, it's more a spirit!

After a quick break we set off again and in no time the lake became wider and the water crystal clear. It felt more like being on a river because of the fast flowing current with the little canoe fighting against the waves and the water spraying all over us.

Time for the umbrellas to come to our rescue. We forged ahead slowly, and in the excitement of it all we hadn't noticed that the sun had gone behind some ugly black clouds; it had become dark and soon started to drizzle. The umbrellas were now really being challenged between horizontal and vertical!

Soon the drizzle turned into a downpour with almighty thunder and lightning and the boat starting rocking ferociously. It was frighteningly dark and visibility was down to a few feet.

Major seemed unperturbed and had every intention of pressing on but I was a mere chartered accountant from London with a big interest in self-preservation, so I urged him to head for the nearest land. After a bit of persuasion he relented and we turned towards the shore.

We were relieved to reach dry land. It was almost pitch dark and all we could see through the intermittent flashes of lightning was a dark old monastery building looming in front of us. As we approached we saw that it was full of children peering curiously out of the windows with others standing on the veranda to see who these approaching strangers were.

We headed for the door but Major beckoned us to keep going for a few minutes, despite the lashing rain, until we reached another smaller monastery building. Standing at the entrance dressed in old saffron robes was an unusually tall, well-built and handsome monk; he was probably in his early fifties. The monk urged us to enter. He welcomed Major, who he obviously knew, and invited us to come in and sit down. We sat on the floor facing the monk. In no time some novice monks produced hot green tea and some typical savoury snacks (the equivalent of our chunky crisps). The refreshments were most welcome.

The monk was eager to find out about us all and when MuMu spoke to him in Burmese he was extremely impressed and fascinated because he had assumed she was a foreigner.

He particularly wanted to know about MuMu's family in Taunggyi. We chatted for one hour or so and he told us that this village had been slap in the middle of operations involving both the Pa'O and the BCP during the insurgencies and as a result had been constantly harassed by the military. The government had cut off all aid to the area and even now they lacked even the basic amenities.

I was still curious about the children in the dark old monastery. The monk understood my question in English but chose to reply in Burmese.

What he told me changed the course of my visit, and my life.

"We have some 500 children in these monastery buildings; some orphans, some abandoned and some from the poorest families. We have adopted the orphans and look after, educate and feed all of them."

The rain had stopped, the skies had quickly cleared and the sun was out again. Our host agreed to show us around. I was about to see something quite remarkable and impossible to describe.

The monk took us from one building to another, perhaps five in all, in different stages of disrepair but all spotlessly clean. Children attending various classes occupied every room in every building. They were all used for schooling including the dark old monastery.

"During the day these are all classrooms and at night they become sleeping quarters for the children," explained the monk. "Children are entitled to one box for their belongings."

We could see the boxes were neatly stacked up at the side of the room. All of them exactly the same shape, size and colour. We finished the rounds of the various premises and talked to several of the children, some who surprisingly enough perhaps, could understand a little English. The place was immaculately clean and the children looked happy and were well behaved.

As we continued our impromptu inspection, we came across several monks sitting outside a shed peeling vast quantities of pumpkins, onions and other vegetables.

There were several open fires with huge pots and a few industrial sized rice steamers behind the shed. Some ladies were cooking and a lot of youngsters were helping out too, grinding chillies and herbs and adding a selection of local ingredients.

Our guide explained how this was a very small fishing village and they were all volunteers who regularly came to help cook and feed this army of children.

We were observing a village where most of the residents were children. Major whispered as we walked that the monk – U Thu Wona – had been handed just one orphan at the height of the insurgencies twenty years ago. U Thu was himself a young man at the time but adopted the child and had brought him up with the help of a village lady. He'd begun to educate the boy.

The rest is history. More and more children began to arrive and over the ensuing years the monastery with its boarding facilities had become increasingly popular, not just for the high level of formal education provided, but more because of the way their education was uniquely blended with a Buddhist upbringing.

People from surrounding towns and villages who couldn't afford to bring up their children were among those seeking places. U Thu never turned anyone away and before long the monastery was caring for more than five hundred orphaned, abandoned and destitute children.

I realised I was in the presence of a truly charismatic person and in the midst of something really remarkable.

The sun was emerging through the clouds as U Thu walked us to the jetty and, as we were about to bid farewell, he asked if there were any suggestions we would like to make to improve the facilities for the children. There was no time for a considered response. All I could think of was that it would be amazing if these children could be given access to computers.

He smiled, paused and replied: "Most of these children have not seen a computer let alone used one. We do not even have any electricity."

U Thu had triggered something inside me. I thought about everything we had, about the luxuries we take for granted. And then I looked at those children. Yes, they were happy. But their dreams were yet to be realised. I knew I had to do something. I knew I could and I knew I would.

U Thu sensed correctly that he hadn't seen the last of me. He smiled. "See you very soon," he said, "you are most welcome to come and stay with us." Because of our diversion we had no time to travel further south and instead decided to head for lunch and then back to the hotel where we arrived late that same evening.

I couldn't sleep at all that night and tossed and turned trying to fathom a way to help those children. Obtaining the computers seemed simple enough but I would still need to overcome the challenge of how to charge the batteries given the lack of mains electricity in the village or anywhere in that vicinity.

The next morning I started making local enquiries about how to lay my hands on some generators. Solar charging panels were a possibility but that seemed more like an option for a bigger power project so I abandoned that idea.

After searching around on the Internet, I found what I thought would be the perfect solution. Samsung had recently launched a solar-powered computer. Bingo!

I thought it would be worth finding out if they were prepared to donate a few for a worthy cause which would earn them some good publicity, given the status of Myanmar as an emerging country where there was likely to be a huge demand for high tech products.

"Have compassion
for all things,
rich and poor alike;
each has their suffering.
Some suffer too much,
others too little."

Buddha.

Chapter 12:
Take Me To Your Leader

The following evening Major came to tell us that a most prominent Pa'O leader was due at the hotel and would like to invite MuMu and myself for dinner. He said that Bo Kyaw had agreed to talk openly and that I would be allowed to reveal his true identity.

I was very excited and after a quick shower and change of clothing I hurried to the reception area clutching my second bottle of scotch in the hope that it would do the same trick as before and encourage free-flowing conversation.

I was ushered into the dining room where Bo was waiting with Major. I offered my gift, which was opened within seconds and served by one of the many waiters who were hovering nearby.

After the usual pleasantries I asked rather cheekily, testing Bo's knowledge of slang, if he was going to spill the beans? There was a long silence, which made me think I may have got off on the wrong foot. Bo took a deep breath and, gulping down an extra-large measure of whisky, began to speak.

"Feroze first of all I must apologise and confess that I am actually not a Pa'O. I am an Intha." (The indigenous people who live around the lake).

There was me thinking I had a scoop: an interview with a notorious Pa'O leader, ready to talk openly for the first time. I composed myself and Bo continued.

"But you see we were all different ethnic people united against a common enemy in the Ne Win Government and we were all fighting for equal rights. It did not matter where we really belonged and when I joined we were all part of the SURA anyway (Shan United Revolutionary Army)."

Bo explained how he had married into a different tribe whose family were related to the Pa'O. Clearly this involved lots of different tribes and ethnic groups joining forces to make common cause against the government.

"My initial task," he continued "was to encourage the Intha people to join the Pa'O movement but I failed spectacularly. Being devout Buddhists the Intha were content to live their self-sufficient and peaceful lifestyle and were not prepared to resort to any form of violence."

That explains the calm and peaceful ambience we felt at Lake Inle, I thought.

Bo took another large gulp of whisky and began to tell his story.

"I was sent on lots of different combat missions including spending a year on the Salween River where I contracted malaria. Major saved my life by smuggling me to a hospital across the Burmese border into Thailand. I am sure I wouldn't have survived otherwise." He glanced at Major appreciatively. "After that I had to give up combat duties. We suffered several casualties at Salween, notably doctor Sabai's brother who was fighting with us at that time.

"My next challenge was to mobilise the funding for the organisation. I selected a unit of a dozen or so officers whose job was to work among the Pa'O people with the sole purpose of collecting taxes to fund our activities.

124

"Each family was expected to pay the equivalent of $2 a year – despite this they remained loyal to the cause and protected my men who were told to take flight rather than fight if they came across any government soldiers.

"The money raised was used to buy guns and ammunition as well as other vital supplies that were mainly sourced by Major during his regular smuggling trips to and from Thailand.

"We lived in the jungle in hiding for at least twenty years and I only managed to see my family for a day or so every three months."

Since the truce and fresh elections, Bo has become the chief financial officer for the group of hotels of which Inle is one. He's also a member of the central Pa'O committee and when once that would have earned him a jail sentence at the very least, now it's a requirement to represent the party in political circles.

Dinner was now being served. But rather than the normal hotel fare, Bo had arranged for us to enjoy some home-cooked food that MuMu had been reminiscing with him about earlier. It was kind and generous of him.

On our next trip I learned a lot more about Bo Kyaw who had a reputation among the local people here as a swashbuckling maverick PNO commander. In the early days of the insurgency he would ride around the mountains and the lake areas on a white horse, as if he was the Lone Ranger out troubleshooting.

Bo was married to Sheila, an elegant and well-respected local teacher, who he'd met when she came to Inle as the first teacher at the Pa'O boarding school. Bo Kyaw was in charge of setting up the school on behalf of the PNO.

He swept Sheila off her feet but despite her family's close connections with the PNO they didn't approve of the relationship thinking – probably quite rightly – that Bo was a high risk. So instead the two of them eloped.

When Bo first volunteered to join the PNO they were suspicious because he was an Intha. In those days it was common for every insurgent organisation to be infiltrated by spies from either the government or rival factions. It was the only way to gather intelligence given the lack modern forms of technology.

So the PNO asked Bo to prove his allegiance.

He achieved this in spectacular fashion by kidnapping the Mayor of Inle (a senior government appointee) and holding him to ransom, only releasing him when the authorities agreed to free some very important PNO prisoners. After that Bo became a wanted man with a price on his head and pictures of him were posted everywhere.

Not only did Bo prove his allegiance to the PNO beyond doubt but he also became an instant hero which fast-tracked his progress within the organisation.

Bo had been typically coy and somewhat modest about his role within the movement during our previous conversation. The intervening years had obviously mellowed him and now as a grandfather much of his work involved political lobbying and encouraging charitable work on behalf of the Intha and Pa'O people. He had ended up following in the family tradition. His father had been the first doctor to be sponsored by the local Nyaung Shwe council and had spent all his working life looking after the lake people. Like father like son, Bo was continuing to serve the community.

MuMu wanted to visit her relatives in Taunggyi so the next day we headed off overland in a jeep that Major had organised. As we drove over the mountains we met a truck crammed full of soldiers. We could see they were armed and possibly on some sort of surveillance exercise.

They clearly recognised our jeep (it carried Pa'O markings) and acknowledged Major as if he was a superior officer. There was an exchange of pleasantries, the army contingent saluted Major, and we continued our journey. I was curious about why Major was so friendly with the soldiers given that he had spent most of his life avoiding the army.

Major smiled. "They're former Pa'O soldiers who joined the national army after the peace process," he said. "They're actually part-time reservists."

So where, I wondered, would their loyalty lie in the event of another uprising involving the Pa'O? I guess we won't know unless that happens, but my suspicion is they'd continue to side with their communities. Given the brutality of the past and such deep-seated resentment I also wondered how the peace settlement had been achieved. Had the PNO sold out?

With his customary smile Major explained. "On one of my teaching visits at the monastery in Inle I received a letter from U San Aung who was a middle ranking civil servant in Yangon. Since U San was originally from Taunggyi he was well known to me and well respected in the community. The letter included an invitation to meet up to discuss a possible peace deal.

"Although this wasn't a high level approach it was a smart move on the part of the authorities, putting up someone with established grass-root contacts who had credibility within the local community.

"I set out immediately for Taunggyi but decided to stop along the way to get a feeling about the mood of Pa'O village leaders towards a possible change. It was clear that the Pa'O were battle weary after two decades of fighting and so finding a peace settlement on honourable terms was clearly going to be welcome. I reached Taunggyi three days later."

At the meeting Major was convinced that the authorities – the ruling State Law and Order Restoration Council (SLORC) – were keen on reaching a settlement and invited the PNO leadership for more formal talks with the Council in Yangon.

Major reported the outcome of his meeting to the PNO Chairman U Aung Kham. U Aung Kham Hti was a former monk and Burmese politician before he became Chairman of the Pa'O National Organisation (PNO) and head of its military wing the Pa-O National Army.

On April 11 1991, the PNO, headed by U Aung Kham Hti, agreed a ceasefire with the ruling SLORC represented by General Saw Maung. The PNO was granted a number of business concessions as well as control over some territory in the southwest Shan State, which later became known as the Shan State (South) Special Region-6.

Major continued. "I kept a low profile and didn't attend the direct talks but remained on hand in Yangon being consulted from time to time."

Many other ethnic groups made peace at the same time including the Karen, Kayan and some Shan groups. But a few continued their demands for separatist status, notably the Kachin. There have been reports since of fighting along the Chinese border around Maija Yang. News agency reports talk of a Kachin army of some ten thousand armed with antiquated rifles and slingshots fighting a losing battle with government forces.

128

The Kachin were being pushed out of Myanmar into China as refugees. But as far as the Pa'O goes, the peace agreement has been welcomed. It's had a profound effect on village life. For the first time in twenty years they've been able to lead normal family lives as the men returned from the jungle to resume their previous peaceful occupations.

And once again the government began to fund education – building new schools and hospitals and infrastructure projects including much-needed roads and bridges. As well as the obvious benefits from a peace agreement, it also included provision for members of the Pa'O army to act as a volunteer border force albeit under the command of the Myanmar army.

But what really made the difference was the government's initiative to pump money into funding a jobs programme that included support for new business ventures and training. The idea was they would be run as co-operatives with the workforce recruited from among the Pa'O people and any profits would be ploughed back into the community.

U Aung Kham Hti

"Work out your
own salvation.
Do not depend
on others."

Buddha.

Chapter 13: Land Of Opportunity

There were several such initiatives but two in particular are worth mentioning and, surprise surprise, they both involved Major. The first involved the government leasing some recently discovered ruby mines at Mai Hsu in Shan State to the Pa'O in partnership with some other groups. Given that production at the country's most famous Mogok mines near Mandalay was coming to an end, this was a shrewd move on the part of the government to ensure mining went ahead there and that the operation was profitable.

Historically, Mogok had been the most important source of rubies. The deposits there had been mined since the fifteenth century. The finest jewellery houses used Mogok rubies because they possessed the most sought after characteristic, a vibrant red colour known as 'pigeon's blood'.

Whilst the Mai Hsu mines didn't possess such high quality stones, the deposits were so large that it was hailed as the most important discovery for centuries. The rubies from these mines tended to be lighter in colour with a slightly bluish or purplish hue, which wasn't deemed as attractive as the deep uniform coloured rubies from Mogok. Invariably those from Mai Hsu ended up being heat treated to make them more attractive but the process also diluted their value. Nevertheless these mines re-established Myanmar as a major source of rubies.

And while the mines provided much needed employment the profits were limited because the stones could only be sold to the government at controlled prices.

Major was appointed 'operations director' at one of the mines. Needless to say he found a way to maximise profits by setting up a lucrative freelance enterprise on the side in which he and his business partner, who put up the money, managed to hive off some of the best stones that they then sold on the black market in Thailand. Major used the money to support the communities.

The second business opportunity was sheer genius. Major had kept in contact with U San Aung (the civil servant who initiated the peace deal). On one occasion when Major and U San were admiring the beauty of the lake, U San had said how amazing it would be if travellers were able to visit and stay there. Therein were sown the seeds of the first hotel on the lake. U San had a friend, Kenny McLennan, a Scottish architect, who visited Burma on a regular basis.

On one such visit U San and Major asked him about the possibilities of designing and building a hotel and whether he was prepared to undertake the project. Kenny agreed and Major put the plans to the Pa'O council for approval. After much deliberation they were approved, but at half the size originally proposed.

Major was appointed the building director. The inspiration for the design came from the local Intha village huts that were constructed from bamboo and woven straw. There were many problems that had to be overcome; the biggest obstacles being the lack of electricity and drinking water, which was still a problem in 2009.

Funding the project and sourcing the right materials was also a huge headache. The government provided a modest grant which helped pay for some of the fitting out. But finding the raw materials for the actual construction was a different matter altogether.

Major embarked on a fund raising roadshow going from village to village securing pledges for bamboo and other building materials. Where families couldn't afford to donate materials they invariably offered their services as labourers. Then, before even half the structure had been completed Kenny McLennan died. That's when cousin Ting stepped in and finished off the project. The hotel opened for business in 1996.

As promised, the very first dividend to the local Pa'O community came in the form of jobs at the hotel. Major had already earmarked some of the smartest and brightest in the villages but they still needed training. There were two basic roles that needed filling – general hotel staff and entertainers.

Finding locals who could provide first-class service was easy because their Buddhist upbringing ensured they were naturally polite and mild-mannered. The second requirement was the ability to entertain guests, which meant a willingness as well as an ability to sing, dance or play some form of musical instrument.

So began the tradition, which remains to this day, where every evening the staff put on a dance and music show at dinner – moving seamlessly between cooking, serving and performing on stage.

The hotel provided impetus to a tourist boom at Inle, which has since become one of the country's top holiday destinations. More than two million tourists are expected to visit Myanmar in 2014 and most will include a trip to Lake Inle. There are now several luxury hotels and spa resorts in the area but demand still far outstrips supply, especially in the peak season between November and February and it's essential to book many months ahead to guarantee somewhere to stay.

After a week or so at the lake we took a flight to Thandwe and to my favourite beach resort of Ngapali Beach. We were a bit worried about our safety following the violence between Muslims and Buddhists in the state.

The problems stem from successive governments treating members of the Rohingya Tribe (originally from Bangladesh) as illegal immigrants, though many have lived in Myanmar for generations. To be accepted as citizens they have to prove they settled prior to 1823 – which of course is virtually impossible given the lack of records.

The religious tension between members of the Rohingya Tribe, who are Muslims, and the Buddhist Rakhines erupted into full blown and bloody street battles leading President Thein Sein to declare a state of emergency and impose martial law. This threatened to undermine the country's progress towards democracy and damage its international reputation. Fortunately the beach area remained peaceful and we reached it safely.

"To understand
everything
is to forgive
everything."

Buddha.

Chapter 14.
All That Glitters Is Not Gold

On my return to London I wrote a formal letter to the CEO of Samsung. I outlined the work of the monastery and asked if the company would consider donating a few of their new solar powered computers to this worthy cause.

I didn't get a reply. So some weeks later I contacted their press office enclosing a copy of my letter and asked if they were prepared to help in any way. I immediately received a short but polite email saying that Samsung could not assist on this occasion.

I was disappointed but understood their position. However I still needed to get hold of this equipment, which I was now going to need to pay for. But even that proved impossible because it turned out Samsung didn't sell this type of kit in the UK. I kept getting unhelpful standard computer generated responses from the contacts provided on the Samsung website, and there were no other telephone numbers listed where I could speak to a real person. I even tried to find suppliers in the US (the equipment was listed on the Samsung US website) but with no success.

I had hit a brick wall. Sadly there was no way even a paying and willing customer could break through the cyber wall!

In the end I turned to Dwight Lewis, my office's IT man, who took on the challenge wholeheartedly and came up with an alternative solution.

He bought a couple of standard laptops and separate portable solar charging panels specially designed to charge computers and other such portable devices. He also ordered extra laptop batteries and various bits of software to make it all, hopefully, work!

It was now March 2013. A November visit was just too far away even though November to February is the most pleasant time to visit as the rest of the year is either very hot or very wet because of the monsoon. May was the earliest I could get away from work, so MuMu and I decided to brave the heat and go then. I emailed Major if he would ask the monk U Thu Wona – or Phongyi as he was affectionately known – if we could come and stay at the monastery for a week or two to teach the children how to use computers. I had also bought some interactive DVDs to help teach the children English, maths and spelling as well as basic computer skills. I included a backup – a selection of Mr Bean DVDs just in case we failed with the computer course!

Major promptly confirmed that the monastery would be expecting us, so we started making preparations for our trip to Inle and in particular to the school and orphanage at Phaya Taung.

Our tickets had been booked and Major had made the necessary arrangements. He also said he'd like to stay at the monastery with us which was a huge relief as we didn't quite know what to expect when we got there.

As Chairman of the Mayfair office of Crowe Clark Whitehill, chartered accountants in London, I enjoy a degree of flexibility as far as these things go; but an unexpected work commitment suddenly came up which put the whole trip in jeopardy.

I had been advising a high profile and extremely wealthy male client on a very acrimonious divorce matter in which the financial settlement hinged on where he was domiciled for tax purposes.

It was either France or the UK. In the UK the courts are notorious for ruling in favour of the wife, usually on a 50/50 split of wealth, which would cost my client £50 million. However, if he could prove he lived in France then the courts were likely to award her a tenth of that amount. So there was a lot at stake.

I was being pressurised by his legal team to be available as an expert witness but the case was scheduled for the time we were supposed to be leaving. I agreed to produce a written witness statement but there was still every chance the other side would want to cross-examine my testimony and the judge could well subpoena me to attend.

In the meantime news reports about Myanmar revealed that the violence between Muslims and Buddhists had spread from the Rakhine Region to the Mandalay Region in the centre of the country. There were reports that at least thirty people had been killed in the rioting and of many charred bodies left lying on the streets of Meiktila, a city not far from Mandalay. About six thousand Muslims in Meiktila had been forced to flee their homes and were seeking refuge at a stadium on the outskirts of the city.

On March 22 2013 the President declared an indefinite state of emergency in four townships in the Mandalay Region – Meiktila, Wundwin, Mahlaing and Thazi. There were even rumours that the violence was spreading towards the Muslim areas of Yangon.

This was dreadful news, and a serious setback on the country's path to establishing a more liberalised state. Nevertheless the EU announced the lifting of all economic sanctions (but not arms sanctions) and Myanmar lurched a little further along the bumpy road to democracy.

While we waited I used the time to try and decide how best to go about teaching the children. Although I am accustomed to using computers this didn't mean I had the faintest idea how to run classes. What I needed was some inspiration.

For now the immediate task was to become familiar with the teaching software, ensure all the equipment was fully charged and hope that there wouldn't be a problem clearing customs into Myanmar.

We had:
◊   Two laptops
◊   Two iPads
◊   Two solar panels
◊   Two additional computer batteries
◊   Two camera /batteries
◊   An iPod and mobile phones
◊   Mobile wi fi
◊   Memory sticks
◊   An assortment of English and maths teaching DVDs plus various other DVDs including Mr Bean, the Wizard of Oz and Bugs Bunny!

I still hadn't had a reply from Major as to his whereabouts and if he was going to be able to join us. I was becoming worried when he finally emailed to say that because of his own security (and hence our welfare) he would ask either Ting or Bo to escort us to the monastery. He had already made sure our favourite boatman would be available.

I was really disappointed because I needed to spend some time with Major so I could fill in the missing pieces of his story. I wrote to him again urging him to reconsider. However I did not receive a reply and, as we were about to fly to Yangon the following day, I panicked.

I felt an urgent plan of action was needed, as all email communications seemed to have failed – which can often be the case – or they'd been delayed due to censorship or just lost in Myanmar cyberspace. I decided to use the old fashioned telephone. While foreign mobiles don't work in Myanmar, local landlines and mobile phones can at least receive overseas calls.

So I began by calling up the various hotel numbers I had for Major but no one was picking up, probably because the time difference meant the offices were closed. Eventually I managed to get through to the Naung Shwe transport office that provides boats and taxi services for the hotel at Inle. Fortunately the manager recognised my voice and gave me Major's personal mobile number.

Major gave me the good news that he was going to try his very best to finish the job he was doing and catch the same flight as us to He Ho, but he couldn't promise. He would call us when we arrived at our hotel in Yangon with an update on his plans. However, he said that there were "far too many government observers" so we needed to be discreet.

In the meantime, the situation regarding my client had been resolved, as the judge in the case couldn't accommodate a private session to hear my evidence ahead of the hearing. I guessed that my evidence wasn't important or crucial enough for him to subpoena me. I wished my client the very best; gave him some advice and left it to his QC.

We boarded the flight for Yangon on April 25th still unsure how the trip would pan out. Thankfully we had no trouble getting our equipment through customs and checked in at our usual hotel.

After a short rest we took a taxi to Scott's Market (now known as Bogyoke Aung San Market). It was midday and fearfully hot. MuMu and I wanted to buy some Shan clothes – loose baggy pants and shirts for me and sarongs or longyis, as they're known in Myanmar, for us both: the latter so we could preserve our modesty when changing in communal areas especially at the monastery.

Major still hadn't made contact with us so mild panic set in again. We waited. He turned up later with some Pa'O friends having tracked us down to the hotel bar. I couldn't help but notice how out of place they looked compared to the comparatively fashionably dressed crowd in Yangon.

We ordered some cold Myanmar beer and chatted. For a moment I thought he was suspicious about our motives for being there and wasn't convinced we were serious about the computer classes. Maybe this was why he seemed reluctant to accompany us? But, after talking for a while, he seemed to change his mind.

He said he would only book his ticket when he got to the airport in the hope there'd be no time for airport security to check names. If all else failed he would hop on a coach, which would take at least seven hours, and meet us at Inle. I was relieved – with Major at our side everything would work out just fine.

Ting called later that night insisting that he would like to pick us up at He Ho airport and drive us to Inle. He wanted to show us the intense development that was taking place around the lake.

As we had already booked our transport we arranged to meet a couple of days later at the hotel. For the first time we had a free day in Yangon so MuMu and I hit the tourist trail.

I picked up the hotel brochure and read the section on Yangon: "Myanmar has been called The Land of Gold, and that is not surprising at all when you consider just how beautifully the capital city sparkles. Giant, golden and glittering pagodas will take your breath away in this friendly city. Also, Myanmar is well known for its lovely jewels. In the heart of capital city Yangon, the Bogyoke Aung San Market offers travellers a stunning array of jewel choices. Here they will find gold, rubies, sapphires, jade and other precious stones sold by the thousands. All other manner of hand-crafted goods are available too, to delight any shopper. Myanmar is a densely populated land with a population of approximately 48 million people. The capital city of Yangon itself boasts a population of five million. The people of the land are predominantly Buddhist, though there are many other ethnic groups represented."

Having traipsed around the Scott Market, which we always enjoy, we decided to visit the city's most famous landmark – the Shwedagon Pagoda. It's one of the great wonders of the world. The country's most deeply revered religious shrine and an astounding and magical monument: a golden dome, which contains eight hairs of the Buddha, is topped by a spire that stretches hundreds of feet towards the stars.

We had asked yesterday's taxi driver to come and pick us up at ten that morning before the heat of the day took hold.

I had previously resisted a visit believing it was an opulent tourist trap, but MuMu rightly insisted. The taxi driver dropped us at the entrance and

suggested we leave our shoes in the car. As we walked into this awesome place I heard the soft footsteps of a young Burmese girl approaching. She politely beckoned towards a pay booth suggesting I may wish to make a contribution of five dollars.

MuMu spoke to her in Burmese and, assuming she was my guide, she then said only one of us had to pay. A bargain on two counts because the ticket also included this history:

"The origins of Shwedagon Pagoda materialised in brilliant epoch in Buddhist history over 2500 years ago. In India Prince Siddhartha had just attained Buddhahood when two brothers, Tapussa and Bhallika, merchants from Myanmar who offered a gift of honey cakes, visited him. In return the Buddha personally removed eight hairs from his head and gave these to them for enshrinement in their native town of Okkalapa, which is now the city of Yangon." On their return the two brothers presented the Buddha's hairs to the King of Okkalapa who erected the Pagoda and enshrined the eight hairs together with the relics of the previous three Buddhas. "According to legend, when the King opened the golden casket in which the brothers had carried the hairs, incredible things happened:

"There was a tumult among men and spirits... rays emitted by the hairs penetrated up to the heavens above and down to hell... the blind beheld objects... the deaf heard sounds... the dumb spoke distinctly... the earth quaked... the winds of the ocean blew... Mount Meru shook... lightning flashed... gems rained down until they were knee deep... all trees of the Himalayas bore blossoms and fruit."

The Pagoda was originally just 66 feet tall, but from the Fourteenth Century onwards successive monarchs added to it or re-gilded it until Shwedagon reached its present height of 326 feet. It has ten different sections: the base, the three terraces called Pyisayan; the Khaung Laung so called because of its bell shape; the Baung Yit with its distinct embossed bands; the Thabeik meaning 'monks food bowl'; the Kya-lan, an ornamental lotus flower; the flag shape vane which revolves to the direction of the wind and the Seinbu, diamond bud. The Hti, the Hngetmana and Seinbu are decorated with 3,154 gold bells and inlaid with 79,569 diamonds and other precious stones. It proved a memorable distraction.

As agreed we waited for Major at the hotel. We were in danger of missing the flight when he called to say he would meet us there, which meant a last minute dash. We arrived just in time.

It was an enjoyable trip and gave me time to catch up with Major. Along the way we stopped to take this picture:

Soon we were on the boat heading for Inle. I felt a real sense of calm, a truly peaceful feeling as though I had returned to where I belonged. Sadly though there was no repeat avian symphony to serenade us – they had already migrated for the summer to greener pastures. Ting often joked and called me a 'son of the lake' because of the manner in which I had fallen head over heels in love with this place and its people.

We were all tired and Major had some work to do, so we had a quick dinner and retired for the night.

Ting, Sabai and cousin Lette arrived the next afternoon. As usual Bo Kyaw had laid on a feast for us, though on this occasion it was more in honour of his friend Ting and his guests. Afterwards Ting and Bo said they wanted to show me a modern day catastrophe that would change the face of the lake and the community forever.

Bo had been restoring his jeep which dated from the Second World War, and the boys piled in with Bo driving and Major in the front passenger seat, both wearing US army caps while Bo also had a pair of binoculars around his neck. I imagined them exactly like this in their military days.

Bo drove up the east side of the lake and it wasn't long before we all had a good view of what was happening. It was sheer devastation. The entire base and one side of the mountain had been bulldozed and flattened for development. Bo explained how enough land was being sold to build a hundred new hotels with a capacity of more than five thousand rooms.

The current capacity of five hundred rooms already placed a strain on the fast dying lake and this looked as if it could be its death warrant.

Dramatic measures were going to be needed to ensure that the river system and springs that feed the lake didn't become polluted with pesticides and other chemicals. I read in the Myanmar papers that the UN had offered to help preserve and restore the polluted areas of the lake but that politics was getting in the way of it happening.

Perched on the top of the hill, Bo and Major shared the binoculars as they surveyed the area, pointing here and there while discussing how best to lobby politicians to save their beloved lake. At least this crude invasion of concrete couldn't take away the beautiful golden sunset that was, paradoxically, enhanced by the dust from the excavations. It turned the light into a hazy dark red glow. Perhaps the sun was expressing its own anger. That evening Bo organised another dinner party, which was accompanied by more whisky and a bottle of local sauvignon blanc, but it was hard to get into the spirit of the occasion given what we had just seen.

It was a difficult and sensitive issue for the local Intha and Pa'O. While not wanting to stand in the way of progress, which would boost tourism and thus their standard of living, they were also wary of any development which would ruin the very thing the tourists came to see. Unless the construction was undertaken in an environmentally sensitive manner, and with due respect to the local people, it would be disastrous.

The PNO needed to adopt a different approach to this battle. This was one that would be won by negotiation and diplomacy rather than the gun. I worried whether these former guerrillas were armed with the right credentials to fight this type of battle in the political minefields of Naypyidaw, the country's new capital.

"He is able
who thinks
he is able."

Buddha.

Chapter 15: Logging On

We set off after breakfast early next morning. There were two boats as Ting, Sabai and Bo personally wanted to see us settled in at the monastery. We took some cartons of juice and protein bars with us knowing we were going to be on a vegetarian diet for the next week or so.

The water levels at some parts of the lake were really low following the dry summer season and only the skill of our boatman, with an occasional helping hand from the young boys swimming alongside, enabled us to get through. This was also a rewarding way for the youngsters to earn some tips.

After three hours or so we stopped at Samkar and headed for the monastery. Within seconds we were surrounded by food and more food – bowls of rice, cooked vegetables, different savoury snacks and of course green tea. We were joined by what must have been the village leaders. This was no ordinary welcome. I worked out that it was because Bo Kyaw was with us.

The villagers had been complaining about the lake weed which was choking the area and making it impossible for them to use their boats. Bo had successfully intervened on their behalf lobbying the local authority through the PNO to clear the growth. Now the villagers wanted to thank him. Needless to say there were clearly other issues to resolve and Bo listened attentively.

After an hour or so we adjourned to the restaurant for lunch. On the way and as we were passing a collection of ancient stupas, Ting took me by the hand and showed me how these monuments were being destroyed. Ruined not by the ravages of time and natural erosion, but by the obsessive manner in which the local people had tried to restore them. This involved covering them in cement and applying cheap gold coloured paint. They believed that repairing the stupas would please their God and guarantee them a better place in the afterlife.

Ting showed me one six hundred year old stupa that he had lovingly restored with the help of local craftsmen. It included beautifully painted walls and ceilings with a magnificently restored teak roof. But even though he had pleaded with the local people to look after it, nothing had been done. He realised in despair that he was fighting a losing battle. Pleasing Ting wasn't going to earn them the rewards that a fresh covering of cement and cheap paint would!

After a short walk we arrived at a new restaurant. It was owned by Bo's niece who had married into the now infamous family responsible for producing the rice wine – and many headaches! The young couple had been told to expect us and we enjoyed an enormous feast that was particularly welcome given the meagre rations we could expect at the monastery. We took the opportunity to wash it down with more rice wine knowing we were definitely going to be deprived of alcohol for the next few weeks.

After lunch we headed straight for the monastery at Phaya Taung, which was another hour away. The lake here was wide, deep and crystal clear – a complete contrast to the northern part, which was rapidly becoming overdeveloped. Our small craft struggled through the waves, spraying water all over us. But we were all well equipped with umbrellas and waterproof jackets. We held the umbrellas in front of us to protect our legs from getting soaked. This was certainly no pleasure cruise.

There was a complete absence of activity on this part of the lake except for thousands of wild birds feeding in the fields bordering the banks.

With no computer teaching experience and virtually no understanding of the language, I was going to need a great deal of luck and help to make this trip a success. As the boat lurched onwards, I prayed for further inspiration.

After a fairly hairy journey and a good soaking we finally got to Phaya Taung. Just as we arrived an idea came into my head.

We were greeted by Oo Pazin, the deputy head monk, who was waiting for us with some teenage students who helped carry our kit up to the monastery.

Half way there we got a glimpse of what life here was really about. Sitting under a large red blossom tree was a little boy perhaps five years old.

He was wearing an old blue t-shirt with a pair of dirty shorts and was completely engrossed in eating a bag of sweets. He was clutching it as if his life depended on it. Somehow he seemed out of place.

Oo Pazin said something to him; but he didn't look up or answer. He was completely preoccupied and, on closer inspection, clearly agitated. Oo Pazin saw the shock on our faces.

"This boy arrived here two days ago," he said. "We don't know his name so we call him Mayawk (monkey) affectionately. He has no parents and doesn't speak either Burmese or Pa'O. He is traumatised. He is a Lisu (mountain tribe). We have adopted him and we give him anything he wants. But all he wants are sweets, so we give them to him."

I didn't ask Oo Pazin what had happened to his parents, I asked Major a few days later instead. He told me how hundreds of desperate young people had been illegally making their way across the border into Thailand as economic migrants. Completely unaware of the dangers of sexual disease too many of them contract AIDs.

Destitute illegal immigrants have no access to medical facilities and when they return to their own villages, often seriously ill, they don't get proper medical help there either. The result is that many of them die.

We were taken to the monastery where the monk who's affectionately known as Phongyi made us all feel at home. Bo, Major, Ting, Lette, MuMu and I sat around Phongyi in a semi-circle. We were served the ubiquitous green tea and snacks. I was keen to get going on setting up our project, but Major indicated for me to hold back and wait until the right moment.

The monastery was supported by the PNO, and Bo and Phongyi obviously enjoyed a close working relationship. The fact that Bo was with us was a clear endorsement of our good intentions.

After a general chat, I felt the right moment had come to broach the subject of our role. Through Major, I asked Phongyi if he had any particular ideas or instructions about how he wanted us to conduct the classes. But he said he was happy to leave that to us. We had brought two laptops from London and acquired access to two secondhand ones locally so I suggested we taught the children in classes of around eight at a time. Say ten-year-olds for two hours in the morning and two hours in the afternoon. I felt the younger ones were more likely to pick up the basics faster than the older ones. Eventually, all being well, the youngsters could become the teachers.

Phongyi liked that idea but also suggested that we taught the older students, aged between eighteen and twenty, because they were likely to stay on either in their villages or at the monastery as teachers. He thought we could begin at eight am and finish at six, which meant we could also fit in a two hour class for the other children in the morning and afternoon. No chance of slacking here, I could see!

He realised we must be tired, but first wanted to show us around the school and the classroom we would be using. There were a few separate buildings including the old, now abandoned, monastery. We realised that some of the buildings served as classrooms during the day and dormitories or eating areas at night.

Phongyi finally took us to the room set aside for our classes. It was fairly spacious with a white board, a row of tables and twenty or so chairs. On either side of the desks was a row of about a dozen keyboards along with some empty boxes stacked in a cupboard. It seemed that these had been recently donated but that was the extent of the equipment. What the room lacked in sophistication it made up for with an amazing view of the lake.

We had been honoured to have been assigned one of the best available spaces. It was late afternoon and time to bid farewell to our escort party – Ting, Lette, Sabai and Bo. I am not sure why, but they seemed a bit down as we walked them to the jetty. On reflection I think it was because they were worried we'd never survive outside the comfort of the hotel!

We were shown to our quarters, which were in a building at the far end of the monastery. Downstairs was a sort of open basement area where all the food and other supplies were kept.

On the ground floor, where we entered, was a longish room some fifteen by thirty feet, which was used as a dormitory during the night and a dining area during the day. It contained a table, several plastic chairs and not much else. An area about six feet by twelve had been partitioned off for us. This was where we'd be sleeping. Our beds comprised a double blanket laid out on the floor. We were really fortunate that Major had arranged to bring us fresh towels and a clean white sheet but the real life saver was the mosquito net which our boatman rigged up around our sleeping area protecting us not only from the rampant mozzies but also from all sorts of insects and creepy crawlies, particularly lizards.

At the other end of the room there was a similar space that Major would share with the boatman and one or two students. There was one Western style toilet cum bathroom. When I say bathroom, it was a hosepipe that led to the balcony for us all to use. Having later surveyed the whole place, this was a comparative luxury!

We left our bags in our room and made our way to the classroom where we set up the computers, solar panels, and additional batteries and generally got a feel for the place, mentally preparing ourselves for the next day. I felt pretty good about things.

We had managed to get here in one piece with all our gear and everything had been lined up for us to get cracking. Time to log off for the night.

As we were walking towards our living quarters, the deputy head monk Oo Pazin approached and asked if we were comfortable. He pointed us in the direction of a magnificent old Bodhi tree on the side of which stood an open shelter. As it was such a nice evening he suggested having our dinner there with Major and the boatman.

And so began our routine. Four or five smiling young girls would appear, chat to MuMu in Burmese and serve our dinner... which three times a day for the next seven days was more or less the same meal: rice, a watery vegetable curry, a cooked vegetable dish (whatever was available) and some pickled fruit or vegetables such as green mango, mustard leaves or edible flower buds. There was always a plentiful supply of green tea and bananas. Sometimes we were served fried peanuts as a source of protein.

I discovered later that other than on special occasions the children had to be content with just rice and the watery vegetable curry; the other food was reserved for the special guests. Oo Pazin said the girls who were waiting on us would also attend our first class the following day. It gave us the opportunity to get to know each other. It was a happy evening and I could feel a genuine sense of serenity and kindness. Oo Pazin bid us good night and said breakfast would be served at six.

We were exhausted and slept really well, completely oblivious to the insects and lizards that shared our sleeping quarters. From that night on we began to get used to and even embraced living with the creatures around us. Often I would find a lizard or two peering at me through the bed sheets as I woke. But the mosquitoes were something else.

Life at the monastery began at sunrise, which for the monks meant rising at four a.m. for meditation and prayers. We awoke as the sun began streaming into our room. The sounds of the monastery's gentle comings and goings could be heard intermingled with birdsong and the noise of various domestic animals. I realised that we were actually in a very remote place, which until twenty years ago had been a jungle where tigers and other wild animals roamed. Nature's choir was telling us that morning had broken.

So we were up around five and quickly headed to shower and get ready but the children were ahead of us. They were already chatting excitedly on the steps outside the building's entrance, peering in occasionally to see if we were ready.

Soon we were joined by Major and the three of us were served a hearty breakfast, but we could barely manage a mouthful. We were excited, but in a nervous way!

What we really needed was a cup of that strong local coffee we were used to back at the hotel. We knew the children would have high expectations and we didn't want to disappoint them.

Slightly ahead of schedule, we headed to the classroom and soon were joined by four novices, boys and girls all somewhere between eight and ten years old. They were accompanied by Phongyi, Oo Pazin and several

other adult teachers who sat at the back of the room watching and waiting for us to perform miracles! The children sat in front of the computers, fiddling, waiting to get going. This was it. No turning back now. Time for my master plan.

MuMu (my talented artist, photographer, translator, guide and long-suffering wife) began by drawing a large house on the white board. She followed my instructions and drew a gated entrance, a lock on the door, and several rooms with filing cabinets. She had no idea what I was attempting to reproduce here but thankfully she had enough faith in me to keep going.

When she'd finished the drawing I told the children (through MuMu) that they were about to enter a magnificent English country house. But to get into it they would have to switch on the computer (press the start button) walk towards the door and open it with the key (password) and enter. They could go into any room: the maths room (Excel) or the English library (Word), the drawing room (Paint) or the mail room (Outlook). They could open a cupboard (the programme) and having used the contents they could keep them by storing them (Save) in a filing cabinet (Folder).

The children grasped the concept immediately and it helped them find their way around the computer's functions effortlessly. Using the mouse was a little awkward at first but they soon got the hang of it after a bit of guidance and practice.

By the end of the session they all knew how to open the computer, access the programmes and close them properly. Oo Pazin (who was also in charge of education) was very enthusiastic about my concept of a magical house. During the afternoon session we introduced the children to the various DVDs so they could work on their own and practice using the mouse.

The same approach worked for the older children, so at this point I realised we only needed one syllabus, which I drew up along the following lines:

- ◇ Day 1: Introduction
- ◇ Day 2: Word
- ◇ Day 3: Excel
- ◇ Day 4: Paint
- ◇ Day 5: Outlook (and merge Excel / Word/ Paint)
- ◇ Day 6: Presentation by the students
- ◇ Day 7: Closing

MuMu also used the time to teach the children how to type as there was an abundant supply of redundant keyboards! The younger children also enjoyed the DVD maths, English and spelling exercises whilst the older children were more interested in honing their practical work-related skills, such as preparing CVs or producing budgets for fledgling businesses. But all in all, the younger group got a handle on things much faster than the older ones. One particular ten-year-old novice had completed much of the course and was totally proficient in all the Microsoft office programmes within two and half days!

As the course gained momentum more and more people joined in as observers and often the other teachers came and helped – learning in the process. Visiting relatives peered through the windows in astonishment at what their children were doing. And so from a class of eight with two sharing a computer, now three were sharing with a mixed group of onlookers and helpers joining in. On each occasion we would have between fifteen and twenty people in the room. Lessons took on a life of their own.

The children were so keen that we hardly had time for lunch and rarely finished before seven. The children either arrived early or stayed late practicing, that's if they were lucky enough to get their hands on a computer with batteries that hadn't run out by then.

What was truly remarkable about the children was not their aptitude or gratitude or even their keenness to learn, but the manner in which they conducted themselves. They not only showed us how dignified and courteous they were, but also how caring and considerate they were to each other; always willing to share and ensure everyone got a fair go.
We also started befriending one very curious visitor. Mayawk (the monkey) would come to watch us through the window but persisted in asking Oo Pazin for money to buy sweets.

MuMu asked Oo Pazin why he pandered to Mayawk's constant demands for sweets and why he, and indeed everyone else including the other children, indulged Mayawk's every demand.

Oo Pazin explained the Monastery culture. "At this time Mayawk is very vulnerable and his greatest need is all the kindness we can offer; we certainly do not wish him learn how to shout or get angry – this is not our way. Soon, but only when he is ready, we will move on to only rewarding him when he has completed his tasks, for example his studies or chores. In the fullness of time he will observe and adopt the ways of kindness and consideration that the other children practice. But for now we need to win his confidence."

Never a word was spoken to him in anger or rebuke. By the end of our stay we began to see some remarkable changes in Mayawk's behaviour. He began to communicate and understand Pa'O, he would smile and was clearly happy though he still kept up his demand for sweets. Although now he was much more patient and prepared to wait for them. He stopped peering through the window of our classroom and would come into the room. He took a particular interest in my iPad rather than the PCs – clearly this was a boy with taste!

Generally, the children began to enjoy the lessons more as they learned their way around the computers and would be waiting for us outside the classroom to greet us with songs of appreciation and high fives! We were being swamped by kindness.

One of the exercises we asked each student to complete was to write an essay about their life and experience at the monastery.

Here is one story exactly as it was written.

"My name is Ma May Than Nu.

I live in Pha Yar Taung. I reached here at 2004.

This village has many wonderful places.

In this village all the people are very kind and help good relationship with me.

My grandfather's name is U Sam Mya and my father's name is U Maung Than. He is a farmer.

I have made many friends, when I reached in Pha Yar Taung. Among them, my best of my friend is Ma Saw Myint and she is very kind and relationship.

She is fatherless child and a poor girl.

She always helps many people."

And this is what she told us about her background.

She was born in the village of Hti Wa Mu in the Nyaung Shwe Township. Her grandfather, although a Lisu, joined the Pa'O insurgents and was a fellow freedom fighter with Major. Her grandfather was wounded during the fighting and had steel rods inserted in one of his knees. Thereafter he had difficulty walking and eventually died from an infection.

Her father was a farmer in a small village with a population of about a hundred. There were six children. Three of her younger sisters had died; one from malaria when she was just two, and the others in a fire at home. May Than survived because she and her mother were visiting an aunt in another village.

The tragedy tore the family apart and eight years ago May Than was handed over to the monks in the hope they could help rebuild her life and provide a better future. She had recently passed her exams and was hoping to train to become a nurse.

The days flew by, as we were always so busy. On a couple of occasions I managed to escape for a walk around the local village with Oo Pazin but even that was rushed as the girls were already waiting to serve us dinner. As soon as we had finished eating Phongyi would join us and we would talk late into the night, which meant we were always totally exhausted by the time we went to bed.

One such evening we were discussing the course and giving an assessment of the children's progress. Of the twenty or so students who ranged in age from eleven to twenty, by far the most accomplished was an eleven-year-old called San Aung.

Having never even opened a computer before, he was working through Microsoft Office programmes on day two, so after less than ten hours of tuition, he was an expert. When I introduced him to the Paint programme, he became equally proficient in no time at all. He was brilliant at everything he did.

I asked Phongyi about him. "He could the next President of Myanmar," he smiled. "He is a truly remarkable boy, well ahead of the others."

Apparently San Aung's parents got divorced when he was about three. He went to live with his father while his little brother went with his mother. But his father soon abandoned him and he ended up being taken in by the monastery. Now he's training as a novice monk.

About five years ago when he was eight he'd asked to see his mother again. The monks managed to trace her and arranged the visit. After a few days with his mother San Aung decided to return to the monastery and asked to bring his younger brother. Phongyi said he could, but only if his mother came too.

I did not understand the full significance of that until Phongyi told me this story.

"Once upon a time a young man saw a very handsome monk having a bath and thought to himself that if I were a woman I would really marry this man. The power of the monk made this man's wish come true and he became a woman. But he was a married man with children so he could not go back home as a woman so he disappeared. His family thought that he was dead.

"He began to live like a woman and one day she met a woodcutter. They fell in love and the woodcutter took her to his village and they got married and had children.

"Some years later some villagers from where she had once lived were visiting the woodcutter's village and she recognised one of them so she asked about her family. The visitors were surprised when she told them that she was asking about her wife and children. So she explained that once she had been a man and that even the woodcutter did not know about her past. But she desperately missed her old family.

"The visitors told her that she should go to this handsome monk and ask for his forgiveness. She found the monk and asked for forgiveness and she became a man again.

"Lots of people asked him what it was like to be both a mother and a father. He said that a mother carries her child for nine months, breastfeeds and look after the child. There is simply no comparison between the love of a father and the love of a mother for a child. There is a unique bond between a mother and child."

The course ended with a presentation by each of the older students about to pass on the skills they'd learned to the younger ones. This was pretty impressive and we could see that at least four of them had real teaching potential. We thought we were at the stage where the ability of the students and their eagerness to learn computing could form part of their curriculum. It would certainly help them find jobs and at the very least equip them for the future which, even in Myanmar, was becoming so dependent on technology. We now needed to get hold of another ten or so computers so that every child had a chance to learn.

At the end of the course, Major presented all the students with awards. The only things we could buy at the local shop (half an hour away by boat) that would make suitable prizes were torches for the boys (there was no electricity) and sarongs for the girls. MuMu organised a special bag of goodies for Mayawk – no, not more sweets, but a set of clothes, some shoes and some basic school essentials including pencils and erasers. This was his passport to attend the classes.

Phongyi thanked us before asking me to address the students. I wasn't prepared for that so I did my best to improvise.

I said that a human being learns all the time and that the old do not always teach the young. The students had learned some computer skills from us. But we had learned a lot more from them. We had seen them behave with humility, kindness, generosity and with the utmost dignity at all times. We should aspire to learn how to live by their example.

"Your work is
to discover your work
and then with all your heart
to give yourself to it."

Buddha.

Chapter 16: Phongyi's Story

I had been very impressed by the way the monastery was run and how efficient, motivated and relaxed everyone appeared to be and, dare I say it, how happy they appeared to be. I felt there were lessons we could apply to our often chaotic and stressful way of life back home.

In the meantime, I felt I needed to understand the man before I could understand his teachings, so I asked Phongyi if he would be prepared to discuss his own background.

He said he had a natural reservation towards self-publicity but would think about it and let me know the next day.

Phongyi agreed to tell his story and for the next six nights the four of us – MuMu, Major and I sat up every night talking with him until the small hours. We were exhausted. We had to be up at five in the morning, while Phongyi would probably get up at three thirty. But we all knew this was a significant occasion: he was honouring us by sharing his story, so we grasped every second we could.

Phongyi began his story. "I was born on the July 4 1958 in the village of Pinlaung Township which is in Shan State at the foot of the Pa'O mountain range near Loikaw. There were only five houses. My family was extremely poor; my father farmed a bit of land at the foothills of the mountains and we barely survived.

"When I was fifteen months old my mother passed away from malaria, complicated by some water-borne disease. I was the youngest child with one sister and an elder adopted son. My father told me that I longed so much for my mother that he had to console me by pretending to breast feed me. It was the only way of comforting me. I was too young to be left alone at home so he took me to the farm in a basket on his back. To balance the weight he put some cow dung on one side of the basket.

"When I was eighteen months old my father remarried someone who already had a son. My stepmother became like my real mother but in the abject poverty in which we lived we all had to fend for ourselves.

"I remember that as soon as I was able to walk I had to go some 40 minutes to the stream to bathe myself and also bring back enough drinking water for the family.

"The first five years were like a dream but there was the occasional nightmare when dacoits (vagrants) attacked our home; tying up the family members and robbing us of what little we had. Because there were only a few houses in the village we could not provide security and became easy targets for desperate people.

"This was a time when the Pa'O was hugely repressed under the feudal system and these dacoits operated with the tacit approval of the feudal landlords (Sawbwas). There was no school in the village or nearby at that time so the parents got together to open one themselves. They had no funds of their own and the government was not prepared to help because the BCP (Burmese Communist Party) insurgents operated within that region. So the villagers turned to the Pa'O (PNO) leader Aung Kham Hti who helped finance the school and taught students up to grade seven.

"However, the school only operated sporadically because of the internal feuding between the Pa'O and the BCP and because both factions were fighting the government. Consequently the students spent a lot of time taking cover from bullets rather than being taught.

"It was impossible to operate a school under such conditions so it only remained open for a few years and I only managed to finish grade two. At fourteen I was almost illiterate. There was no school nearby but because the headmaster felt that I had some promise he arranged for me to join the Buddhist monastery at Lin Lam (near Loikaw, which was one of the big towns in that region).

"I remember very clearly how I would often sit all day watching the traffic. Bullock carts carrying people and goods and the general hustle and bustle of life there, the people, shops and busy restaurants; all that commotion amazed me. It was an extraordinary contrast with my simple and remote life at home.

"There was nothing in the villages where I came from. No schools, no education – just poverty and illiteracy. My villagers had never even seen a house with a proper roof. I felt I had to do something to help my people in the little villages so that they did not remain so backward and to open up their minds so they became enlightened.

"It is like the footprint of a cow in a puddle; the frog sits in this little puddle and thinks it's his kingdom. There is a whole world outside but my people did not even know it existed."

Pausing, he looked at me: "Go beyond even one's imagination because there is no limit!"

He began to explain how his life took on a new meaning. "When I went to Mandalay and then Yangon with its cars, buses and trains I realised how small Loikaw was.

"I resolved then that the path to enlightenment for my people was education. Before, this was just an emotion in my heart. Now I was beginning to plan how this could be achieved. I thought I could find a way to send some of the young people from the villages to be educated in the city, but I had no money to be able to do that.

"In the meantime (1981-83) I kept making trips to the monastery in Yangon. And when I came back the scene in and around the Pa'O villages was even worse than before. The PNO, which had been one of the strongest guerrilla forces in Southern Shan State, had broken apart.

"The communist element became the Red Pa'O and the original, now much smaller force, the White Pa'O.

"They began warring with each other in their own back yard, instead of fighting feudalism, which was the prime purpose of their rebellion. To make matters worse the Red Pa'O guerrillas began to depend on drug trafficking to finance their activities.

"The result was that many people living between the lake at Inle and the mountains found themselves trapped in a war zone – sandwiched between the Red Pa'O and the government forces fighting communism. Often the only way for me to reach the monastery at Lin Lam was to be smuggled across at night in a fishing boat.

"After completing my monastic education in Yangon at the age of twenty four, I settled at the monastery at Lim Lam. The head monk there was a herbalist and so my first job was to deliver his remedies to the various outlying villages. There were no doctors or any allopathic medicines at that time. I was considered the Red (saffron!) Cross by the villagers.

"The Red Pa'O dominated this area with the other communist parties, notably the BCP, who joined together against the government forces. My villages and our people were caught in the crossfire. The Red Pa'O relied on the scarce resources of the villagers to sustain and feed the rebel forces.

"Villages became isolated because their community leaders were too frightened to travel. The government forces labelled them spies while they were bullied and often killed by the Red Pa'O. Anyone who spoke or acted against them was shot. Eventually all the village leaders were appointed by the Red Pa'O.

"Spying and counter intelligence was rife. I remember one monk by the name of Badim Saung, (an astrologer) from our monastery who was found to be working secretly with the Communists, preaching to the villagers to join his party. He was reported by a government informer in the village and arrested. He was found to be carrying a gun and was jailed for several months. He was also disrobed. When he was released he appeared again with the BCP forces seeking revenge. Anyone who spoke or acted against the Communists was killed. Whole villages were burnt if they were seen to collude with the government.

"I realised that my plans for the school would have to be put on hold and that protecting my villagers was the priority. Wearing the saffron monk's robe gave me armour and influence as a holy man that others didn't enjoy. I fully intended to exploit these privileges for the betterment of my people.

"The mantra I preached was that the villagers should remain neutral and not be persuaded or bullied into taking sides – it wasn't their war. If there were any discussions to be had they should be conducted outside the village. I made the mistake of asking Badim Saung to tell the Communists to keep out of the villages. It proved a fatal mistake – and from then on I was branded anti-Communist and became a marked monk. Even my saffron armour ceased to protect me.

"The BCP told me to leave the village or I would be killed. This was the best deal they would offer me. A mere mortal would have been executed for much less. I didn't want to become a martyr without achieving very much so I decided to leave. But before doing so I pleaded with the four village elders to persuade their people to remain neutral and not take sides. They ignored my advice thinking I was far too young and naive to understand such complex politics.

"I left my village secretly that night in a fishing boat and headed for the monastery in Yangon. I thought long and hard as to whether I should give up my status as a monk and take up arms against the Communists, but I realised that keeping the robes meant that at least I would retain a position of authority within the community and from a practical perspective meant I was able to continue to receive donations.

"While I planned my comeback, life in the village was becoming horrific. A Shan government informer in the village had been exposed by the BCP, which retaliated by torturing suspected informers. This usually involved pouring boiling oil into the palm of their hand so it would seep right through. Whole villages were burnt and some sixty of the eighty families in one area were forced to flee their homes.

"Four of the village elders were publicly executed as an example to their neighbours. The villagers wrote to me at the monastery in Yangon pleading for me to come back. I left as soon as it was possible – two months later after the Buddhist Lent.

"As soon as my boat arrived the villagers gathered together crying over the loss of their husbands and sons and saying how they wished they had listened to me and followed my advice. I told them not to seek revenge but to remain neutral and go about their own business. I said I would do my very best for them and would work to protect them even if it cost me my life. The villagers began to rely increasingly on me for leadership and guidance.

"No one from the village was prepared to stand and be elected as a leader (usually a one year appointment) because leaders were usually the first targets. Instead they began to rely more and more on me for everything; if they wanted to build a bridge they would come to me; if they wanted to build a road they would come to me.

"One of my very first acts was to appoint a leader in every village. This was in the belief that since the appointment was made by a monk, rather than by the government or the BCP, they were likely to be unbiased and also safe because Buddhists fear the wrath of God. This turned out to be the right choice and the village leaders were at last able to make their own decisions again and some normality was restored.

"On one occasion the BCP came to me threatening that if the villagers didn't help to blow up the bridge used by the government to reach the area there would be severe repercussions. I said that we would only do that if the BCP handed in their arms and ammunition. They didn't agree, as you might expect, but there were no repercussions.

"The government kept up its squeeze on the communists by establishing a security ring around the villages cutting off supplies of food and ammunition. As a result the BCP was severely compromised and the army managed to establish a foothold in the mountain areas, albeit at the price of restricting the freedom of the villagers.

"And so some level of safety and stability returned and I was able to turn to my principal goal of establishing an educational programme for my villagers.

"Once again I had to delay my full devotion of prayer to God and instead put all my energies into opening a school, which had been on hold all this time. The political position had stabilised and every moment was precious as the children were growing up fast.

"In 1986 I started work on establishing a primary school in Phaya Taung. I had to go to villages further afield to raise sufficient funds. But persuading them to contribute to a primary school when they were already supporting their own was extremely difficult. The only way to convince them to help was by promising to set up middle schools and beyond as well. On that basis I managed to collect four thousand US dollars over a five year period. It was enough to complete the primary school.

"It began life as an open building with a roof. We had sixty children and over time the walls were built around the flimsy structure. It took another five years to complete the work brick by brick, and by that time the number of pupils had grown to two hundred. Since most of them came from far and wide we provided boarding places for them.

"In the middle of all this, when I was thirty years old, my father became terminally ill. He was seventy eight and lived in a village some miles away.

184

I was lucky to have had the privilege of caring for him in the last year of his life. I went to him every morning; fed him, bathed and looked after him. Each evening I returned by boat to the monastery and worked at the school while my assistant monk (Oo Pazin) took care of things during the daytime.

"The school became well known for its high standard of teaching and I was elected to be the head of the twenty eight school councils in our region. While my role was to lead the development of the educational programme and to ensure the right standards in our area, the people were increasingly relying on me for advice and to adjudicate in their disputes, particularly concerning land, domestic and business issues."

I asked Phongyi how he set about deciding on such delicate and sensitive matters. After pondering my question he came up with another classic example of his voice of reason.

"I didn't make any judgment or ruling. I relied on the 227 scriptures in the Buddhist book of rules as the basis of law. But my method was to make the parties understand the futility of being in dispute. Appealing to their better nature, I'd ask them to reach a resolution amongst themselves rather than having an outsider impose a judgment. That way they were likely to resolve their issues without any loss of dignity."

He came up with a typical example. "Once there was a fight between two villagers at a festival and one of them beat the weaker person until he was bloodied and injured. The case went to the police magistrates who were likely to award the injured party several million kyats in compensation if the dispute couldn't be resolved between them.

"After much deliberation I suggested that the aggressor should pay the other person's medical costs and genuinely ask for forgiveness. The man apologised unreservedly in front of all the villagers. The injured party accepted it gracefully and refused to even accept the medical costs. Justice had been done with dignity and the two of them became good friends.

"During my time as a schools counsellor I decided to carry out some research to discover the educational standards in each village. The idea was to establish the number of young people who had reached a particular grade and chosen to remain in their village rather than going off to the city. I asked the village leaders for the figures but they had no idea. So I went from house to house gathering my own facts and figures. What I found was truly shocking.

"Only one had passed exams at seventh grade, when they were around fifteen or sixteen. The following year – the eighth grade, again just one. And none the following year. Only one passed the tenth grade. No one achieved higher than that.

"I realised that there was absolutely no opportunity for young people to progress in their own villages and that all too often those with any schooling simply left for the towns and cities leaving behind the villages that were filled with uneducated and oppressed people with no future.

"I needed to find a way to provide education to at least the middle grade.

"However, the financial challenge of keeping the primary school going, and particularly finding fifteen dollars a month to pay the two teachers, was always touch and go. There was no money to even feed the children. Although the fighting had more or less stopped, the villagers were pretty well destitute.

"I needed to find a way to raise more money without taxing the people too much.

"At the time very few of the villagers had ever seen a film. So I asked one of my fellow monks in Yangon to buy some Chinese videos, which were readily available there, and to bring them when he next visited us. I managed to borrow a video player. We already owned a hand-operated generator and an amplified microphone used for preaching, which we adapted as a loudspeaker."

The school doubled up as a cinema!

"I gave the loudspeaker to the monk who cooked for the children and asked him to tour the villages by boat drumming up interest in a film show at the monastery. "We charged five cents per adult. The same amount covered two children. We also sold snacks at the show. This initiative was a great success and enabled us to raise just enough money to pay the teachers' wages.

"We weren't out of the woods yet though, and later when things got really tough we would sell anything we could lay our hands on. Apart from paying the salaries, we also wanted to start a fund for the middle school. By now we had a hundred children in the primary school and they all needed higher education. It would have been a tragedy if they had to finish their schooling so soon. So during the course of these film gatherings I lobbied hard for donations to establish a middle school for the villagers' children. I said that the monastery would provide board and lodging, but the parents would have to provide their clothing. This continues to be the arrangement today.

"It was a challenge convincing the parents to allow their children to continue their education when they could be working on the family farm or earning money elsewhere. We also had to convince the children that they would be better off continuing their education. They all had to board because of the distances involved and because there was no proper transport.

"But the biggest challenge was to find the wages for the extra teachers. So I set off with my begging bowl again going from house to house appealing for yet more money and somehow managed to raise another $2000. I then lent it all to a businessman charging interest of $5 a month which, with our other fundraising efforts including the film shows, meant we had enough money most months to pay for seven teachers.

"The middle school eventually opened on June 17 1993. This was also the first year we began accepting orphans and those whose parents could no longer afford to look after them. I could not refuse, and during the next fifteen years or so, more and more arrived as a result of fighting, disease and poverty. We adopted hundreds of homeless and abandoned children, which is how the monastery also became an orphanage.

"It was pretty much hand to mouth every month and on one occasion we were so seriously short of funds that we had to sell our boat to pay the teachers. On another occasion I had to borrow money from a local trader to buy fifty bags of rice to feed the children and to see us through. I myself only had one robe and a pair of old slippers. Times could not have been more difficult and, looking back, it's a wonder how we survived this period without a proper school building, or money for pens, paper or books. This was the position until 2000.

"Although around the turn of the century the BCP had lost much of their influence and firepower they were still in evidence, which meant the government refused to provide funding for any projects. As far as they were concerned, this was still a separatist area.

"As the situation became more stable I urged the PNO to lobby the government for support and in 2004 they responded, providing grants for the school in Samkar as well as for our school. They also built a new hospital, donated a few canoes and built some roads.

"However there was a quid pro quo. The deal with the government was that they would fund the middle school at the monastery and pay the teachers' wages provided we redesignated it as a government school. This wasn't an issue; in fact it was a welcome relief because it meant we wouldn't have to struggle to pay the teachers. The authorities were also happy as it gave them some political brownie points.

"The student numbers kept growing as our academic achievements improved. I next turned my attention to how we could extend the middle school to include high school level exams.

"I asked the government for permission to extend our teaching to years nine and 10. (Class 10 exam levels were examined on a national basis). The government turned down my request and instead suggested that the children could go to school in Samkar. This was far from ideal because of the distance and travel that would be involved.

"The staff agreed to extend their teaching to year nine, but that still left twenty or so students in year 10 facing an arduous daily journey by canoe to Samkar.

"During the monsoon season this was especially dangerous with the surface water on the lake often whipped up by storms and high winds. Risking the children's lives in this way was unacceptable. But there was no alternative and so we had to do it for a year. But only one of the children passed their exams.

"After that and for the next few years we arranged for them to lodge at various homes in Samkar. The pass rate jumped to 80 per cent. But this wasn't sustainable from a financial point of view. As the number of children at grade 10 increased, the cost of boarding fees in Samkar became untenable. We had to do something to justify our claims that we could provide an education from grades one to 10 and that the children could finish with their national school exam certificate.

"I continued to lobby for improvement to the monastery's facilities through the PNO. It did not succeed. Now I felt I had no other choice but to try myself. I made my way to the Ministry of Education offices in Mandalay. I was shunted from office to office and nobody even seemed to have a record of our existence let alone anything else. Clearly this was hopeless. It seemed unlikely that there was anyone there with the authority to make such a decision.

"I returned to the monastery thoroughly disheartened, but not yet willing to give up.

"There was only one place left to go and that was the central Ministry of Education in the new capital, Naypyidaw. But I prepared this time. I copied all the papers I had about our school, all the official permissions, awards, correspondence and letters of reference. I went to pray at the most sacred Buddhist temples in Bagan and Mandalay. I prayed and prayed until I got to Naypyidaw:

"God of all beings; parents do not wish to see their children in trouble; keep them safe, educate and enlighten them."

I interrupted. Why didn't he pray for help to get permission for his school?

"Only God knows if permission for the school is the best outcome for the children," he said. "It is best to pray to God for him to provide the best outcome for the children – whatever that might be. Pray with all your heart, mind, body and soul. You should be true to your word and if your prayers are granted you must fulfil the purpose for which you prayed. That is true conviction and faith."

So why not ask for even more?

"I can only ask what is within my worth to ask. For example, if I ask to become a Buddha I have to have the ways and convictions of a Buddha. That is impossible for the vast majority of us as it requires unimaginable sacrifice and worship: not to walk in case you hurt an ant or a creature of God; to fast without swallowing even your saliva and so on."

He continued his story. "I arrived at the ministry but couldn't even get through the front gate. I was stopped and turned away, but at my third attempt the guard relented and called the office. Someone there gave permission for me to enter.

"The office building was spacious and well laid out. I was taken to see someone in the schools department dealing with our area. He knew all about our school and its history and didn't even ask me to show him any papers.

"I presented my case, particularly the difficulty of the class 10 children having to stay in Samkar, and explained that all I was asking for was an extension to our existing school license and enough money to pay the teachers. I wasn't asking for a new school. The official smiled and said he understood the position and would recommend that the committee approved it. It all seemed very easy.

"I was naturally very happy and thanked God. Then I waited for official confirmation.

"Some months later there was an announcement by the Ministry of Education granting permission for a number of organisations to operate schools up to grade 10. There were only three named on the list and ours was at the top. This was one of the greatest moments of my life. I had fulfilled my promise to all the poor villagers who had put their faith in me and donated money they could ill afford. The future education of our children was now secure.

"By now there were four hundred and fifty students enrolled at various levels."

"So what of the future?" I asked.

"We are always stretched for funds because more and more children wish to join the school. We do not stop anyone from coming. When the school opens we will have at least six hundred students. We still have to find the means to accommodate and feed them. It costs a huge amount of money. I am hopeful that both you and Major will work with me so that we can find a solution."

"The mind
is everything.
What you think
you become."

Buddha.

Chapter 17:
Phongyi's Words of Wisdom

While Phongyi told us about his life and work during one of our late night talks, I asked his advice about how best to deal with issues that everyone has faced at one time of another. Here are some of his answers.

Anger management:

Feroze: The monastery seems so remarkably calm and serene. It runs like clockwork with never a word spoken loudly let alone in anger – how do you achieve that and how can we apply these lessons in running our own business?

Phongyi: In my sermon every day I give the same guidance: you have the freedom to say anything, but never make another unhappy by what you say and by what you do. I tell them to think clearly, speak clearly and do your job clearly.

Otherwise, other than study time, everyone is given a rota that covers kitchen duties, cleaning, and other housework. There is also a system of financial accountability.

Feroze: What if the job doesn't get done?

Phongyi: If they complete their duties their job is done. If they do more than their duties, it is praiseworthy.

Feroze: But what if they still do not finish them?

Phongyi: Speak to them without anger. Anger breeds more anger. If they still do not fulfil their duties, you should repeat what you have already said. If their actions do not change they are asked to go back to their village and to their own fate.

Feroze: In a business setting, a stressful environment; surely controlling anger is more easily said than done?

Phongyi: Anger is the product of greed so you need to keep in check your greed to control your anger. You make mistakes when you are angry and make the other person unhappy. You set a bad example because you create a culture of blame. Exercise forgiveness. We all make mistakes.

For example, the businessman wants more money so he wants his workers to work harder and longer. If they don't meet their targets, he gets impatient and angry. Anger is not the solution to productivity. It simply breeds resentment and unhappiness, which is counterproductive.

Do not be greedy and you will control your anger. Your business will be peaceful and will prosper and so will your family and all that are around you.

Success:

Feroze: What attributes are required to succeed in business or indeed in any endeavour? What part does hard work or luck play in its success or otherwise?

Phongyi: If you want to succeed you need to use all your god-given faculties and make your own luck.

196

Here is what I believe is a recipe for success:

- ◊   Vision – Visualise your final goal.
- ◊   Heart – Make your commitment.
- ◊   Mind – Think through your options on how to get there. Choose intelligently.
- ◊   Work – Smart hard work; patiently build a strong foundation one brick at a time.
- ◊   Luck – Make your own luck by doing good deeds.

There are two friends. The first one believes in doing good deeds to make his luck. The second one believes in Kismet (predestined fate). One day the two friends are travelling through a forest and a storm overtakes them.

The first one, who believes in doing good deeds, is hit by falling fruit. The second, who believes in fate, is nearly hit by a falling tree under which he finds a pot of gold.

So the second friend said to the first – look I am luckier than you because it was my fate to find the pot of gold and in spite of your good deeds you only got a handful of fruit.

They went to the astrologer who told them that the first friend was meant to have been struck by a bolt of lightning but he was saved by his good deeds. The second friend was actually meant to have become a king – he was unlucky to have only found a pot of gold. You can change your destiny by good deeds but it is not always known.

Kindness and Self Preservation:

Feroze: In work as in life you sometimes have to get on with different types of people. We can't just tell them to go away if we can't make the relationship work.

Phongyi: A man was travelling from one town to another through the jungle. He gets lost on his way and falls into a 10 foot ditch. A large monkey who has been watching sees him trying to get out but he can't because the ditch is far too deep. The man is desperate to escape before nightfall fearing that otherwise some wild animal would kill him. The monkey says to the man: "I will carry you on my back and I will leap out. But just to make sure that you don't get hurt let me practice first with some heavy stones."

The monkey does this successfully several times and so asks the man to get on his back. He jumps out safely.

The monkey is very tired and says to the man: "Let me sleep in your lap for a little while to rest."

The man watches the monkey go to sleep and thinks that he has nothing to bring back to his wife – why not kill this monkey? The meat will be a good present to take her. He takes a stone and hits the monkey on the head but the monkey jumps up and, bleeding from the wound, escapes up a tree. The monkey says: "I was kind to you and rescued you and now you are trying to kill me?"

The man tries to find his way home but goes round in circles becoming lost, hungry and tired. The monkey takes pity on him and throws him some fruit. He sees he will die in the jungle unless he finds his way home. So the monkey tells the man: "I will show you the way out as I move from tree to tree but I will not come down. Follow the drops of my dripping blood and they will lead you home." The man follows the monkey and reaches home safely.

So you see you can always do business and be kind and courteous even if this is not reciprocated. It is important to fully gauge the other person's shortcomings so you can ensure that no harm comes to you.

Death:

Feroze: Thousands lost their lives in the numerous uprisings. How did you console the bereaved families – especially when it involved the loss of a child?

Phongyi: Once there was a very rich old man who had lots of gold and silver but overnight it all turned into coal. He asked the village elder what happened and was told that his luck had run out. The village elder told him to go to the market and sell all his coal.

Everybody in the market made fun of him; this rich man selling coal. But a very beautiful woman sees that he is really selling gold. The man says to the beautiful woman "I will give you jewels if you marry my son" and so she does and the coal turns back into gold.

His son and his beautiful wife are very happy together and have a lovely baby boy who is the apple of their eye. The old man feels that his luck is changing. But one day the baby boy dies. The old man runs around desperately with his grandchild in his arms to the palmist, the clairvoyant, the herbalist and says to them that he will give all his gold to anyone who can give back his grandchild's life; they cannot. He reaches the temple and asks the monk. The monk tells him that only the Buddha can give him life and points him to a man sitting in the corner of his monastery.

The old man goes to the Buddha and in desperation asks if he will give life to his grandchild. The Buddha says that he can only restore his life if the old man can find at least one household that has mustard oil and where they can also say that there has been no death in their family. The old man runs from house to house. Most offer him mustard oil but none can confirm that there has been no death in their household.

He realises that luck can restore material wealth but nothing can bring back life. He buries his grandchild and accepts that in everyone's life there is death.

In Buddhism we are punished in this life for our misdeeds from this or a previous life. But you can negate your past misdeeds by doing good deeds in this life.

This is a story about a holy man who was very close to the Buddha. He was a very gifted man who could see and hear everything, the past as well as the future, and he could read everyone's mind.

One day, one of his enemies put a high price on the man's head and hired some murderers to assassinate him. But of course every time there was an attempt on his life he could see it coming and disappeared. After many such attempts he asked himself if he had done some wrong in his past life. He knew he had murdered his mother. So he resigned himself to accepting his fate and was finally killed.

His past misdeed was so heinous that no matter what good he did in this life he could not negate it.

Feroze: So is that how we should judge people? He deserved to die despite being so good in later life?

Phongyi: Judge the person by his actions now and in this life and do not condemn him for his wrongdoings in his previous life. His previous life only affects him and it is a matter for him.

Feroze: So what is the purpose of life?

Phongyi: Life is short; master the art of living rather than the fear of dying. You have lived only when you have lived for someone else. If you have lived only for yourself you leave nothing of value behind. What good has your life been?

Feroze: So the message is that we should make sacrifices for others, and that way we will be forgiven?

Phongyi: The sacrifice and good work a person wishes to do should be with full desire and honest intent. It should come from the heart. The real reward is during your own lifetime for your good work.

"Just as treasures
are uncovered
from the earth,
so virtue appears
from good deeds
and wisdom appears
from a pure
and peaceful mind."

Buddha.

Chapter 18:
Divine Inspiration

One afternoon Phongyi asked us to take a slightly longer lunch break so he could show us around the monastery grounds and take us to a local village.

One of his followers collected us in a four-wheel drive. During our inspection of the monastery land we were politely and gently asked if we had any suggestions about ways of capitalising on any of the natural assets. With my business experience, could I see a way of achieving an income from the land to help pay for the upkeep of the school and orphanage?

The plan was to have a general look at things before discussing the possibilities after dinner that night along with Oo Pazin who would be taking notes.

The particular area Phongyi wanted to show us contained a natural hot spring. The unkempt land was mainly used as a thoroughfare for cattle.

After dinner, we sat down as normal to talk, but this time I was acutely aware it was my turn to perform.

My view was that we needed to find a way to make the school and orphanage as financially self-sufficient as possible rather than them having to rely on donations that were precarious at the best of times. This meant starting some form of profitable business venture, ideally one which would also provide employment for some of the children when they finished school, assuming they wanted to stay on. There were several possibilities.

Phongyi's reputation, or brand in business terminology, was key to this proposed enterprise. The community revered him so anything he endorsed was likely to sell as long as it maintained a consistently high standard.

I realised that the monks didn't have the time or experience to organise and run another business that, above all, would have to be run along highly ethical Buddhist principles based on benefiting the community. There were many boxes we needed to tick.

Taking all that into consideration I drew up a list of possibilities:

◇   Developing a hot spring spa.

◇   Opening the monastery as a spiritual retreat including meditation and yoga.

◇   Using the buildings as a natural cold storage facility for the farmers' fresh produce.

◇   Developing a range of herbal products under the monk brand.

◇   Using the natural spring to produce bottled mineral water.

After a great deal of debate we settled on a clear front-runner: natural bottled water.

Not only would this provide great health benefits for the community by reducing illnesses from water-borne diseases, but it was also wholly compliant with Buddhist principles. In Buddhism water symbolises purity, clarity and calmness, and reminds us to cleanse our minds and attain the state of purity.

And to cap it all if we could make enough money to feed the children then we would be on to a real winner.

The conversation turned to naming the product. I suggested we used a picture of Phongyi on the label but he had a better idea. An image of a novice monk – a Ko Yin. I could picture this in my mind and when I got back to London we produced just that based on a photo MuMu had taken of the Ko Yin monks at the monastery.

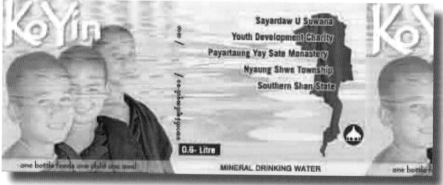

The more I thought about the possibility of setting up a commercial fresh water bottling plant at Phaya Taung the more I became convinced that this wasn't just an impetuous notion but an entirely realistic one.

And if we were right about the branding and it proved a success, we would be able to raise enough money to feed the children every day. I was determined to put my plan in action. My friends and family realised how passionate I was about the project and wanted to help me. But I found it difficult to broach the subject of money without appearing to sound too blunt or too forward. I wrestled with this for some time not knowing quite how to adopt the right approach. I needed their help but at the same time was worried about causing offence.

I trawled the internet trying to gather as much information as possible about water bottling machinery before narrowing it down to one or two possible suppliers. I found one in China who patiently answered all my naive questions allowing me to learn quite a lot about what the process involved. It seemed it wasn't as complicated as I had envisaged and the only real difficulty was the cost of setting up a sterile bottling unit.
'Next, I drew up a list of the challenges. I listed everything except for one thing... how to find the necessary money!'

First, the location. It was vital to establish that the water supply was clean and safe to use. That would require a proper technical survey. Apart from anything else we needed to know that the supply was constant and that the land was actually owned by the monastery and the monks possessed legal entitlement to its resources. They also needed planning permission and to ensure there was the right access to allow distribution by road and/or boat.

Next, the machinery. We had to find the right equipment and somehow get it there and make it work.

Then there was the question of distribution and sales. We were going to have to find someone who knew about that.

We were going to need a lot of luck… And the first bit came out of the blue when MuMu and I were back in London.

Some friends, Asif and Shakiba Rangoonwala, had asked MuMu if she could get them some traditional Burmese ear buds. These are quite unlike the cotton ones available at home.

They are fearsome long thin wooden sticks, a bit like chop sticks, curved at one end to scratch the inside of the ear and with a bird's feather at the other end. Quite why Asif wanted some of these strange contraptions is anyone's guess but it was probably something to do with his late great philanthropic father who was born in Rangoon (Yangon).

So we had been searching for these antiquated objects which sounded to me as if they belonged in a torture chamber rather than a pharmacy. It wasn't easy because they had long been superseded by more hygienic, cheap and efficient versions made in China at a fraction of the price. The shopkeepers either looked baffled or simply laughed at us. Our quest became something of a comical challenge. We toured the city's many bazaars but still drew a blank. Eventually MuMu called her cousin Nyi Nyi to scour the more rural, traditional markets in Taunggyi where he finally found a handful of these precious ticklers!

Back in London the ear buds proved a more than worthwhile investment. Asif was so pleased that when I told him about the water project he immediately offered to help.

He was horrified to learn about the plight of the orphans and the hand to mouth existence of the monastery. I explained what we were trying to achieve and he was instantly won over offering to fund a part of our enterprise through his family charity – The Rangoonwala Foundation.

208

But first he needed a business plan that he could put to the Foundation's trustees. Nothing too detailed, a couple of pages would do, but he needed them in the next day or so. I emailed him our plan and he called me the same evening to confirm he would support the project at the next trustees meeting. He also wanted some more information. This time he needed a feasibility and impact report on the costs of the project and some budgets and sales forecasts. He needed more background information on the running costs and funding for the monastery school too.

I politely told him that a feasibility study wasn't possible given the meagre resources and level of on-site professional advice. There weren't any stats because there wasn't any data. However I said I would do whatever I could to put together the information. I knew I was going to need a lot of help from our friends in Myanmar and it would almost certainly require another trip there including spending some time at the monastery.

It was June 2013 and looking at my office commitments the earliest I could go was October, so I began to make the arrangements and collate as much information as possible before leaving. The first call was to Major to see if he would be around to accompany me and also if he could source the bottling machinery in Yangon or Taunggyi which would make the whole thing a lot easier than having to import it from China.

In London my colleague, Rory St Johnston, had already completed the first draft of the bottle design and wrapper based on MuMu's picture. Meanwhile we set about trying to commission some research into the quality of the existing water supply, and the potential benefits of providing clean drinking water for the people at Inle. Major and Ting were lined up to help on the ground.

With Phongyi praying for us, what could possibly go wrong?

But first, I had some unfinished business. At the instigation of my friend Raj Shah I had written a short paper on our experiences at the monastery including the impact the computer teaching had had on the children, which I sent to a few close friends. Before even asking them for a contribution, I received a number of financial pledges. It meant I was able to order a dozen additional computers from the shop in Taunggyi.

I didn't want to stretch my friends too much at this stage because I knew I was going to need their help for the much bigger and more costly water purification factory.

With the extra computers we had the makings of a well-respected high tech facility along with some expert in-house tutors among the students.

At the end of July I received some encouraging news from Major. The monastery now had a sustainable power source. A benefactor had put up a turbine in a nearby waterfall with the power being fed via overhead cables across the paddy fields to the monastery.

The electricity supply had been tested and was reckoned to be stable enough to power the bottling plant. This was a terrific breakthrough and meant we had overcome one of the biggest obstacles to the project.

Now detailed planning work could begin in earnest. MuMu was unable to join me on this trip as she needed to spend some time with her ailing mother in Karachi. But Major confirmed he would meet me in Yangon at the end of September and be on hand to attend meetings with contractors and suppliers of such things as plastic bottles and labels. I needed to get my head around the manufacturing process and to pull together the financial data needed for the feasibility study. Major's canny business sense and interpreting skills would be invaluable.

The plan was to collect the computers from Taunggyi before embarking on a seven hour car and boat journey to set them up at the monastery. That I hoped would be the end of my involvement in the computers and I could move on with getting the bottling plant up and running. But I was mistaken.

I received a call from Victor Lyons, a renowned expert on multi-language teaching methodology, which he had successfully introduced to many parts of rural India using specialist computer software that he had designed and created. He was in the process of applying to a charity for funding to extend his programme to Pakistan and Myanmar and wanted to talk it through with me. We had worked together before and I had given him some advice and introduced him to people who had been able to help him. When I told him about our computer classes in Myanmar his eyes lit up. It could be the perfect pilot study to support his application for a teaching grant. He asked if I could conduct this for him while I was there.

"It will only take a day or so," he said. Before I had time to consider the implications he said he would send me the software and added: "You have a few weeks to prepare." That sounded ominous.

Events were moving really fast. There was little spare time at the office and my 20 weeks of holiday had already been used up on my various projects in Myanmar. When and how was I going to fit in conducting an educational project along with writing a book, my day job and family life?

I had promised my editor I would deliver the final draft before the summer was out and so I decided the best thing would be to take myself off somewhere without any distractions and bash out a transcript.

I hoped the book would help raise the remaining funds for the water project so it was important to finish it.

Apart from this latest trip to Myanmar, the rest of the year was already taken up with work and business trips. There was so much still to be done.

I was now seriously considering giving up my position at Crow Clarke Whitehill to free up enough time to finish what I had set out to do.

"A jug fills drop by drop."

Buddha.

Chapter 19:
Turning on the Taps

As the plane touched down in Yangon I couldn't help but smile. My first visit had been the beginning of a long journey; along the way I had met many new friends and discovered a new meaning to my life. I had to finish this project.

Major and I spent the next three days talking to various companies that had expressed an interest in supplying various bits of equipment for the bottling plant.

It wasn't easy for several reasons. To begin with I could see these guys wondering about who they were dealing with. After all here I was, a foreigner with grandiose plans to build something I had no experience of. Not only that, but to build it in a remote part of the country. Despite this they seemed genuinely won over. The tipping point was that this was a charity mission involving a Muslim wanting to support a Buddhist monastery.

While they all wanted to help there was only one company big enough to take it on. A director of the company, Kyi Kyi Mar, became an enthusiastic supporter and promised to provide a detailed breakdown of the kit we'd need. In the meantime we said we would deliver water samples for analysis and testing.

Our next mission was to buy the additional dozen or so computers in Taunggyi and deliver them to the monastery at Phaya Taung.

We flew once again to He Ho where Ting collected us and drove us the hour and a half to Taunggyi. Once we'd picked up the computers we adjourned to the hotel at Inle for the night before setting off the following morning by canoe to the monastery, four hours away. This was the beginning of October and the end of the monsoon season so the water level in the lake was really high. The conditions were perfect. We sped along under a clear blue sky. The only problem was I got sunburned!

Our first glimpse of the monastery was of a mass of children all lined up to greet us. Major had rung ahead to let them know when we'd be arriving.

We set up the computers first. The children were so excited that it was a job to keep them at bay while we prepared the necessary power supply. To avoid a free-for-all we decided to organise a system – a computer club. There were two goals. One was to use the computers to help teach them English. The other was to find the right person to take charge and run the computer classes. But before that, I was going to have to teach the teacher how to use the necessary software!

Having done that, I realised we needed to find someone else to actually organise and run the classes. I remembered one of the first students we'd met at the monastery. May Than Nu was one of the older students who'd come on in leaps and bounds and was now teaching some of the younger children. Could she be the person we were looking for?

The next day we got together with Phongyi, the head monk, and his deputy Oo Pazin who was in charge of education, to discuss our thoughts with our new English teacher and May Than Nu. Everyone agreed May Than Nu was the right choice and she immediately set about organising a formal structure based on a computer club. There was no way everyone was going to be able to use the relatively few computers available.

There were 600 children and twelve computers. So it was first come first served – at least to begin with.

Eventually a hundred students were chosen, the idea being others would get their chance once these had attained a certain level.

Having sorted that, we turned our attention to the water bottling plant. MuMu's cousin Ting had agreed to supervise the design and construction of the project which included the site survey and finding a way of piping the water to the plant we were going to build. The water source was only half a mile from the monastery but it involved a tortuous mud track which even our four-by-four struggled to negotiate. It finally gave up altogether. In the end we all piled into a truck to get there.

Ting came up with a design and system for piping the water to our proposed plant. We collected some water samples which we'd promised to deliver to our lady back in Yangon. To be properly analysed the samples had to be back at the laboratory within 24 hours. This was easier said than done given the distance and logistics involved. It included the four hour canoe trip followed by a seven hour overnight coach journey. And it assumed everything ran to time!

We crossed our fingers and sent the samples off with one of the students so that we could continue our work in getting this plant up and running. One of the things I had to do was complete the business plan for Asif and others who wanted to know we had a viable business before committing any funding. This involved finding out if there was a demand for bottled water from the monastery. We were not alone in wanting to supply water. There were already established companies out there. But would the monk's reputation give us a market advantage? Could we break into the market? There was only one way of finding out and that was to ask!

We were looking at supplying shops and villages in a 25 mile radius. We reckoned there were around five hundred hotels, shops and restaurants selling bottled water in the area around Inle at the time. But given the boom in tourism and the vast number of new hotels springing up as a result of all the new development, this was likely to be a conservative estimate. We hoped to persuade them to not just buy our water but to be willing to pay more for it. That would be a huge help in raising the money we'd need to feed and educate the growing number of children at the monastery. We had come up with the slogan 'one bottle feeds one child one meal'. The question was – would it work?

At the time around five million bottles of water were being sold to these outlets costing between 15 and 25 US cents depending on the size. We reckoned we were going to need to capture at least ten per cent of the market. That worked out to half a million bottles a year if we were going to make enough money to fund the gap in the running costs of the school and orphanage at the monastery.

Having crunched the numbers we felt there was enough goodwill and sufficient commitment to make the project viable. With so many new hotels in the pipeline, we were convinced the position could only improve.

Now we only had to raise $100,000 to build the plant!

Back in Yangon we were anxious to find out the results of the tests on the water we had sent to the lab. We had sent three samples from different locations around the monastery. One was from the open water source, one from the bore well and the third from the mountain stream. What was plain to see was that none of these samples was either pure or even suitable for drinking without treatment.

It meant they were all contaminated to a greater or lesser extent which was hardly encouraging for the people drinking it… and that included the children. Our plant was going to be needed more than ever. I don't think it's an exaggeration to say that it would be a life-saver. Clean and safe water is something we all take for granted but Myanmar still has a long way to go on this issue. The children can hardly expect to live long and healthy lives unless this basic human right is provided.

The design and infrastructure for the plant was all there. The demand for the water was a given and the technical know-how was in place to make it happen.

So much had been achieved but none of it was going to be worth the paper it was written on unless we could raise the necessary funds to build this dream.

I needed to head home and get working.

"Happiness comes
to your heart
through your ways.
Change the way
you behave
and improve
as a human being."

Phongyi.

Chapter 20
Enlightenment

As I pen the last lines of this book, the prophecy that Ahwin made when I first came to Taunggyi echoes in my ears. "If you go to the lake your life will change forever."

And so it has. My time from here on will be spent working for the well-being of the children at the monastery. They have captured my heart and my soul. I hope and pray that my efforts help change their lives for the better too.

We all pursue our own dreams in that quest for happiness. For many of us it can be a frustrating experience as we journey through life's ups and downs. How do we reconcile happiness with the barriers we encounter at home and work? It was something I was anxious to ask Phongyi.

"Happiness," he smiled "comes to your heart through your ways. Change the way you behave and improve as a human being."

"That's all well and good but how do we change our ways?" I asked.

"Have discipline. Have principles in your life. Keep to them.
They are your pillars.

"Be honest.

"Help others.

"Try your utmost in every endeavour."

"But," I asked, "other people sometimes try to stop us from being happy. For example, your boss may give you a hard time, or your partner complains too much!"

"Be patient and do not be angry," he said. "If you have acted properly it is their problem and concern and not yours. Some people do not understand or appreciate what true happiness is because they haven't experienced it. How can we achieve something when we don't know what it is?"

"But everyone can," he said, "because there are different levels of happiness. At the basic level it might be the euphoria you experience from watching a game of soccer or listening to a favourite piece of music. It might be the thrill of going on holiday or the birth of a child. The more meaningful and successful the activity, the higher the level of happiness.

"Helping others through your own efforts can achieve a true level of inner satisfaction and real spiritual happiness. There is simply no limit to the feeling this can give you. It can take you higher and higher until your feet don't touch the ground. And you will want more and more."

"Why", I asked, "do people often do good after a tragedy in their lives – the loss of a near and dear one – rather than be angry with God and become bitter as perhaps you would expect?"

Phongyi replied. "Doing good for others provides relief from their pain – this is inherent in human nature."

His words left me with a lot to think about. And since returning to London I have not stopped thinking about the people I encountered in Myanmar, especially the children. They are the future and they deserve to drink safe water.

I thought about Mayawk (the monkey) and how his life had changed. He is now one of the happiest children at the monastery. He attends school and is doing well.

He still loves sweets, but only occasionally! It seems only yesterday he was a shy and hopelessly lost little boy with a grim past and a bleak future.

And then there was May Than Nu, the student who had told us her own harrowing story. From being a shy, introverted girl, she has blossomed into a confident young lady and a dab hand with computers. So much so that she is now the computer teacher and manages the computer club. Who would ever have thought it?

And our genius pupil San Aung. In just three days he managed to master the principles of computing.

Sadly he has not been in the best of health after picking up a skin ailment that resembled ring worm. It's a condition easily treated, but he hadn't seen a doctor. Like water, we take access to medical care for granted. But when you are living in a third world environment it's a luxury.

I can't help but wonder if his condition was somehow the result of coming into contact with his contaminated surroundings.

What we see may look innocuous enough. What we eat may taste good enough. What we drink may refresh us. But the truth is that for thousands of people nothing can be taken for granted.

There are many reasons to be optimistic about Myanmar's future. Tourism and foreign investment are providing the kind of resources that will change the face of the country forever. But the greatest hope remains etched in the faces of the children who expect so little and who give so much.

"There are only two mistakes
one can make
along the road
to the truth;
not going all the way
and not starting."

Buddha

Postscript

Ko Yin Water
Ready, steady go!

Since arriving home from Burma in October 2013 much of my time was spent raising the US$ 100k needed for the water bottling project. I sent my project proposal to many of my wealthy clients and contacts and received huge encouragement and moral support but not that much by way of cash.

I also started meeting clients and contacts in the publishing or writing business to learn how I should go about publishing this book. I was convinced that it would be a further source of funds particularly as it could open up many more speaking and fundraising opportunities.

Meeting these people was a most enlightening and humbling experience. All this time I had been advising my clients on finance and tax – subjects that I had mastered – and now the roles were reversed as the teacher became the pupil. I had some inspiring guidance from Sadie Jones (bestselling author of Outcast), HM Naqvi (author of bestseller Homeboy), Margaret Holden (literary agent) and Dr Brian Klug, Philosopher (aka Klugie) to name a few.

Finally, using my connections, I was able to send my manuscript to Eleo at Penguin Books and Professor Al Richardson at Pluto Books for consideration, yet I mentally prepared myself to self-publish if necessary.

Alongside fundraising, writing this book and working on the bottling project, I also set up a charity, the Inle Trust (www.inletrust.org.uk). Its objectives are to:

1. Relieve the poverty of the people of Phaya Taung and elsewhere in Myanmar and other developing countries.
2. Provide – or assist in providing – clean water and sanitation.
3. Support existing schools and develop education and training schemes for the benefit of the children.

I couldn't have set up the charity and its website without the invaluable assistance of my secretary, Carmel Cannon, and Dwight Lewis our IT man. They both gave a lot of time and support to its administration. And my employers Crowe Clark Whitehill were hugely encouraging, allowing me the freedom to deal with The Inle Trust charity work.

With the money I had personally contributed and some cash from The Hollick Family Trust and The Eva Reckitt Trust there was now US$ 15k in the charity's bank account. Not bad for a few weeks work, but I was an impossible man on a mission.

My friend Patrick Paul and his partner Nina were on holiday in Thailand and, since they were in that region and were keen to be involved, at their request I arranged for Major to take them to meet the great Phongyi in Phaya Taung.

I knew that as soon as Patrick met Phongyi and saw what was happening at the monastery he would be converted. So one weekend as I was writing fundraising emails – and feeling somewhat despondent – Patrick contacted me and said that he would be happy to partner me on this project and match any funds that I was able to raise for The Inle Trust (www.inletrust.org.uk).

To start with he would send me a cheque for US$ 15k (£10k) to match what I'd already accumulated. Within half an hour of this news I'd booked flights for MuMu and I to Burma as we now had sufficient funds to start the building work.

There was even better news to come. The following week Meheen from the Rangoonwala Foundation confirmed that their family charity had approved the US$ 40k grant. Asif had finally come good! The fundraising concert at the David Lloyd Club in Finchley was also taking shape nicely and in the following week I received several other personal donations. The money was flowing in and soon my thoughts moved from fundraising towards the real mission – putting up the water factory!

As MuMu and I boarded the plane for Myanmar on February 26 2014 I realised that I had two exceptional technical challenges to overcome:

1.   The current advice from the machinery suppliers and the local consultant was to purify the water with a reverse osmosis (RO) process. It would strip out all hardness and nutrients, but the processed water would consequently be devoid of any taste. We needed to find a process that kept an acceptable level of natural flavour and minerals for good health while properly purifying the water.

2.   The second challenge was to work out exactly how we could extract the mountain spring water from its source underground and route it the four miles or so onto the factory site. Patrick, using his engineering skills, had made some drawings on how it might happen. But I had to translate them and team up with Ting our architect and the local engineer to come up with a proper plan.

"The only

real failure

in life is not

to be true

to the best

one knows"

Buddha

My original proposal to Phongyi was to use the mountain spring to create good quality drinking water (with the right amount of nutrients and minerals). This would be made available to the children and the village of Phaya Taung and sold to the local public.

But the mountain spring was four miles away from the site and there were many hurdles to clear. It was tempting to go for the easier option of drilling a bore well next to the site. It would provide a plentiful supply of reasonable water, but because it was close to the lake there was a strong chance that it could be contaminated.

Patrick urged that we stayed true to my original objective of providing the very best quality water. Following his own visit to the monastery he set out the rough technical drawings of how we could extract the mountain water from the spring and pump it to a tank at the factory.

However we were presented with yet another obstacle. The mountain spring water, whilst containing a good supply of nutrients, also contained a higher than acceptable amount of hardness (WHO guidelines).

The gold standard in Myanmar was to use the RO (reverse osmosis) method to soften the water and strip out all the dissolved and undissolved elements. This made the water very clear and increased its shelf-life but with the collateral damage of removing all its natural goodness. This option had been almost universally adopted and so the available water purifying technology was based on this market demand.

This did not achieve our objective of providing quality water. After meetings with several water engineers in Yangon, all of whom were adamant that there was no other feasible method,

I emailed Patrick in despair and said that perhaps it was better to "go with the flow" and accept the easier RO solution. This meant compromising on the water quality. However it was likely to sell better because of the water clarity and longer shelf-life and so would provide more funds for the children's food.

This was a new conundrum: water versus food.

Patrick emailed me with these inspirational words:

> "I still think we should do the right thing even
> if it means setting new and higher standards
> for others to follow."

The next day I turned to my last resort – Kyi Kyi Mar (director of our machinery suppliers). I urged her to draw upon her experience and design a process which would achieve our objective. I reassured her that we were prepared to take the business risk.

After discussions with her own engineers she came up with a process that introduced a more extensive UV and filtration system which achieved much of our objective while retaining the integrity of our product. This was an exciting breakthrough – at least on paper!

Since our last visit to see Kyi Kyi Mar in October 2013 she had been curious about why we – foreigners and Muslim! – had chosen to help Phongyi, a Buddhist monk. So she had made a private trip to the monastery during her Christmas holidays. She was very impressed by the good work the monastery was doing under Phongyi's guidance. As a result she was now a convert and had committed to this project at a personal level.

In the three days MuMu and I were in Yangon we had established the water processing system that we were to adopt, chosen the style of the bottle and suppliers and commissioned the artwork for the bottle wrapper. I was happy that we'd achieved what we'd set out to do.

It was time to put all this into action and begin the project. We packed for our flight to Inle Lake. The plan was to meet up with Ting and Major at the hotel on the lake and spend the night there before heading for Phaya Taung monastery very early the next morning.

March 3 2014 was a momentous day. Phongyi and 20 or so children were waiting for us at the pier. The monk had made sure most of the children we knew were there, which made it an even more heart-warming welcome.

Events moved at lightning speed from the moment we set foot on land. Clearly Phongyi had been thinking and working on the Ko Yin water idea quietly confident that I would deliver.

As we arrived we saw that preparations on the factory site had already started. We sat down and informed Phongyi we were ready to go with the building works. We asked him if we could visit the mountain water source. Within minutes some of Phongyi's ex-students arrived with motor cycles. Ting, the engineer, the mason, Oo Pazin and I headed off on an immensely bumpy four mile ride.

After consultations with the engineer and mason, Ting drew up the instructions on how he wanted them to drill down towards the water source, pump the water to a water tank to the highest point on the hillside and pipe it to the factory site. The force of gravity would take the water down the four miles to the factory.

We returned to the building site and to our amazement found that the building measurements had already been marked out and some excavation work already begun. Much of the plinth on which the building was to stand was already in place. A hundred or so students had volunteered and helped.

Phongyi also announced that it was an auspicious day to bless the start of the building. All the students gathered around and Phongyi asked the four of us; Major, Ting, Bo Kyaw and me, each to hammer a wooden stake at one corner of the building. MuMu was asked to pour clean scented water on these foundations.

Phongyi prayed for the success of the venture.

"You cannot
Travel the path
until
you have become
the path itself"

Buddha

What of the children?

May Than Nu had really grown up and spent time talking to and looking after MuMu rather more like a friend than a student. She was now in charge of the computer class.

San Aung, the genius novice monk, was in top form. Together with the other three novice monks, he was also supervising the students' computer lessons. Each of the four had been allocated a quarter section of the computer classroom.

Mayawk the monkey had given up sweets completely! He could already speak Burmese well and was now one of the happiest kids I had ever seen!

The Making of Ko Yin Bottle

Meanwhile in Italy a leading interior design company (Vina Matos and Anne Herzog of www.matos-herzog.it) had generously donated an original design for the Ko Yin bottle:

Their design was based on an equilateral triangle. This was what they said:

"The equilateral triangle represents divinity, harmony, proportion. In Christianity it is a symbol of the trinity, while in eastern civilizations, it is a symbol of the female.

"The four elements are also represented. The apex at the top is the symbol of fire, if crossed by a horizontal line it becomes a symbol of air, while the triangle with the vertex at the bottom is the symbol of mother earth."

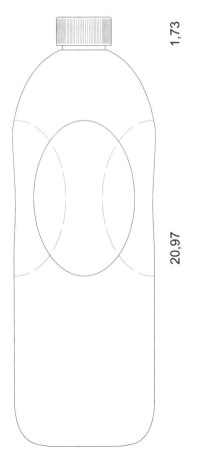

1,73

20,97

Appendix 1: References

1. Lake Inle is a freshwater lake located in the Shan Hills in Myanmar (Burma). It is the second largest lake in Myanmar with an estimated surface area of 44.9 square miles (116km^2), and one of the highest at an altitude of 2,900 feet (880m). During the dry season, the average water depth is 7 feet (2.1m), with the deepest point being 12 feet (3.7m), but during the rainy season this can increase by 5 feet (1.5m).

The watershed area for the lake lies to a large extent to the north and west of the lake. The lake drains through the Nam Pilu or Balu Chaung on its southern end. There is a hot spring on its north-western shore.
Source: Wikipedia

2 & 3. Most of the ethnic minorities in Myanmar live along the country's mountainous frontiers. Karen and Shan groups comprise about 10% each, while Akha, Chin, Chinese, Danu, Indian, Kachin, Karenni, Kayan, Kokang, Lahu, Mon, Naga, Palaung, Pa'O, Rakhine, Rohingya, Tavoyan, and Wa peoples each constitute 5% or less of the population.
Source: Burma Campaign UK.

4. With an approximate length of 2400km, the Salween River is one of the longest rivers in the region. It flows through several countries, originating on the Tibetan plateau in the Himalayas, then passes through Yunnan Province in China, down through Shan and Kayah States in Eastern Myanmar), along the border with Thailand through the States of Kayan and Mon before emptying into the Gulf of Martaban in the Andaman Sea.
Source: Salween Watch.

5. The Burmese Communist Party (BCP) White Flag faction was located in Pegu Yoma while the Red Flag faction was based in Rakhine State (formerly Arakan State). Both were Communist underground groups later assimilated by the government.

6. The Wa National Army (WNA) was headed by former Wa Chieftain Mahasang, and fought for the leadership of the Communist Party of Burma (CPB).

7. The Karenni National Progress Party (KNPP), the largest Karenni (Kayah) group in the jungle, was an anti-Communist group formed following the 1875 treaty between Burma and Britain. The military arm of the KNPP (The Karenni Liberation Army) was involved in an armed struggle with The Burmese Communist Party (BCP), the Kayah New Land Revolutionary Council and The Karenni People's United Liberation Front.

The Kayin (Karen) National Union (KNU) was founded in April 1947, and is the oldest ethnic insurgent group. The military arm of the KNU was The Karen National Liberation Army (KNLA). Its leader was the Mon National Defence Organisation (MNDO) many of whose members, like the KNU, lived in Thailand sometimes joined General Bo Mya.

Source: United States Bureau of Citizenship and Immigration Services-August 2002.

8. Taunggyi is the capital of Shan State, and is the fifth largest city in Myanmar with an estimated population of 205,000 (as of 2010). It is 4,712 feet (1,436m) above sea level.

Appendix 2:

Ethnic profile of Pa'O and Intha people

Burma (Myanmar) is an ethnically diverse nation with 135 distinct ethnic groups officially recognised by the Myanmar Government. These are grouped into eight major national ethnic races:

- ◇ Kachin
- ◇ Kayah
- ◇ Kayin
- ◇ Chin
- ◇ Mon
- ◇ Bamar
- ◇ Rakhine
- ◇ Shan (includes Pa'O and Intha)

These races or tribes are grouped primarily according to the areas where they live rather than by their linguistic or ethnic affiliation, for example the Shan Major National Ethnic Race includes 33 ethnic groups speaking languages from at least four widely differing language families.

Appendix 3: The Pa'O People

The Pa'O form an ethnic group comprising over half a million people. They populate the States of Shan, Kayin, and Kayah. The Full Moon of Tabaung is celebrated as the Pa-O National Day. The Pa'O are largely Theravada Buddhists.

It is believed they settled in the Thaton region of present-day Myanmar about 1000 B.C. They were enslaved, and forced to wear indigo-dyed clothing, to signify their status. Today there are many regional variations of clothing worn.

The Pa'O predominantly engage in agriculture, cultivating leaves of the thanapet tree (Cordia Dichotoma) and mustard leaves. They have largely assimilated into Bamar society, adopting many of their traditions.

The Pa'O legend.

It is said the Pa'O migrated from Central Asia but there is no authenticated record of their origins.

So the legend of Weikja and Naga has been adopted as their ancestry. Weikja was a wise and powerful warrior who could fly through the air and Naga, who could change into a beautiful human form, turned into a dragon when she fell asleep. When Naga came to visit the earth as a young woman she met Weikja. They fell in love and went to live together in a cave.

Naga became pregnant and after falling asleep Meikja returned to find a dragon in his bed.

Heartbroken he flew away from earth forever. When the time came Naga laid two eggs. She gave them to a pious monk to look after. The eggs cracked open and the monk began to peel them to reveal a human body in the form of a boy in one egg and a girl in the other. And so the name Pa (crack) and O (peel) came into being. The boy became the first King of Thaton – the Land of Gold.

Tradition requires that Pa'O women wear two ornaments in their headgear representing the head and eye of the Naga dragon. Their clothing is layered with leggings and longyis (sarongs) under a long shirt and short coat representing the scales of a dragon.

The Pa'O were one of the earliest converts to Theravada Buddhism in South East Asia and remain devout Buddhists.

Pa'O recent history

After the British left Burma in 1948 many of the ethnic minorities in the country began to form groups to promote their independence and to rid the country of the influence of the feudal Sawbwas' gambling and opium dens.

The PNO had already been established in 1946-47 as a resistance movement against the Shan Sawbwas. It later joined forces with the Karen insurgents. In the early 1950s they became the largest insurgent force in Burma operating against government forces in the mountains round Taunggyi and Inle Lake.

A peace settlement was brokered in 1958 in return for the promise of local democratisation. Soon after, all the Shan Sawbwas gave up their powers in return for government compensation. This included a locally elected Shan State Government based in Taunggyi with the authority to raise local taxes and with responsibility for health, education and law.

On 2 March 1962 Prime Minister U Nu was ousted by a military coup putting an end to the development of federalism and democracy. The Pa'O remobilised.

The new leadership renamed the PNLO (PNO) as the SSNLO (Shan State National Liberation Organisation) and recruited troops from other ethnic groups including Shan and Karenni. In the 1960s and early 1970s they enjoyed limited success against government held towns. However Communism was gaining ground at the time, including within the SSNLO, causing an ideological rift between the Communist and Nationalist factions within the party.

In 1974 the Nationalists split from the SSNLO (Red Pa'O) to form the SSNLF (White Pa'O or PNO). Fighting started between these two groups in the Southern Shan State. Villagers were caught between the two warring factions and the government forces. The much-weakened Pa'O became largely ineffective.

In 1978 the PNO established a small military presence on the Thai border near Mae Hong Son funded by bribes from cattle smugglers. In 1983 the SUA (Shan United Army) successfully attacked the PNO camp crippling the Pa'O military and economic activity in that area.

In 1987 the government cancelled certain bank notes more than halving the value of currency in circulation and sparking further unrest.

Many students joined the PNO but could not endure the conditions. Although the Red and White factions within the PNO attempted to settle their differences on several occasions they proved impossible to reconcile with past atrocities.

In 1991 the PNO signed a ceasefire with the SLORC (military government) and in return were able to retain their weapons and local militia. Inter alia, the PNO was also granted mining concessions and agreements to operate tourist hotels at Lake Inle south of Taunggyi.

The PNO is now also a political party with four seats in the Parliament. It is currently working with the government to establish Pa'O self-administration in the townships of Pin Laung and Hshiseng.

The PNO continues to press for improved economic and welfare conditions in the region.

Source: The Pa'O Rebels & Refugees – Russ Christensen & Sann Kyaw.

Appendix 4 - The Intha People

The Intha (also known as 'sons of the lake') are members of a Tibeto-Burman ethnic group living around Lake Inle. They speak an archaic dialect of Burmese and are believed to have come from the Dawei area. They number some 70,000 and live in four cities bordering the lake, in numerous small villages along the lake's shores, and on the lake itself. The entire lake area is in Nyaung Shwe Township.

The population consists predominantly of Intha with a mix of other Shan, Taungyo, Pa'O (Taungthu), Danu, Kayah, Danaw and Bamar ethnicities. Most are devout Buddhists, and live in simple wooden stilt houses woven from bamboo. They are largely self-sufficient farmers.

Most transportation on the lake is traditionally by canoe though more and more are being fitted with outboard motors. Local fishermen are known for practicing a distinctive rowing style involving standing at the stern on one leg and wrapping the other around the oar.

This unique system of sculling was developed so they could see over the vegetation that covers large areas of the lake surface. It is only practised by the men. Women row in the customary style, sitting cross-legged at the stern.

With your help, the story continues
www.inletrust.org.uk